harmonic technique in the rock idiom

the theory & practice of rock harmony

richard bobbitt

dean, berklee college of music

wadsworth publishing company, inc., belmont, california

For the Music Educator

For the Theorist

For Supplementary Reading in Music History

For the Serious Rock Musician

Printed in the United States of America

1 2 3 4 5 6 7 8 9 10—80 79 78 77 76

Library of Congress Cataloging in Publication Data

Bobbitt, Richard, date
    Harmonic technique in the rock idiom.

    Bibliography: p.
    Includes index.
    1. Harmony. 2. Rock music—Instruction and study.
I. Title.
MT50.B65   784   76-12492
ISBN 0-534-00474-1
ISBN 0-534-00478-4 (workbook)

To Lawrence Berk

—persistently explorative

—consistently dedicated

Preface

This book is for the music educator and serious student of rock music. Those of us involved in the teaching and arranging/composition of music in the modern idiom are aware of the need for a comprehensive method for analyzing the harmonic techniques of the music of our time. It is also important to obtain an objective overview of rock chord progression principles, so that they may be examined in historical perspective and related to significant theoretical trends in other harmonic idioms.

European music, in all its aspects, formed the basis of American music throughout the nineteenth century and well into the twentieth century. But as early as the 1890s, a new and original influence began to affect the development of musical styles in America. It grew out of the turmoil, persecution, and physical suffering of slavery. It spread through work songs, folk songs, gospel songs, and the blues. It was a black aesthetic; and with it came "the beat."

The beat in traditional European instrumental and vocal ensembles was a relatively silent expression of inner energy. There was no clapping of hands, pounding of feet, or unrelenting beating of percussion instruments. Black interpretation of the white man's music, however, brought the percussive factor into prominence. The ragtime of Scott Joplin (1868–1917) and others in the 1890s transformed the role of the left hand in piano music into a strong, rhythmically percussive, chordal background for syncopated right hand melodic figures. The drum set became a standard part of even the smallest ensembles, and the first important era in jazz—the Dixieland period of the 1920s and 1930s—featured the interweaving of two or more improvised melodic parts against an extremely strong, percussive rhythmic accompaniment. The percussive element in American jazz-oriented music continued unabated into the swing period of the late 1930s and early '40s, as well as through the "bop" and progressive jazz of the late 1940s and early '50s.

In spite of its important function in ragtime, Dixieland, and jazz music, the beat always served as an accompaniment. In music of the rock idiom the beat came to the fore and dominated the entire ensemble texture. The rhythm instruments assumed a new role of leadership by means of electronic amplification that exceeded the normal thresholds of comfortable sound levels.

The principal performing musicians during the peak years of the rock period—the decade of the 1960s—made little attempt to reach the conventional audiences of the past. Instead, they aimed at those who were ready to cast aside restraint and seek direct empathy with the thoughts, gestures, and freewheeling social attitudes of the players; those who stood ready to reject established patterns and orthodox behavior; those who, consciously or unconsciously, were already part of a rebellion—an irrevocable flood-tide of change that was to affect an entire society. Rock was more than a musical phenomenon. It had become a social and philosophical focal point.

The rock style did not develop as a progressive and logical extension of the era that preceded it—the band era of the 1940s and 1950s. Instead, it erupted. And it cataclysmically revolutionized the generation, transformation, and manipulation of sound. The rhythm section, which had consistently played an accompanimental role in jazz bands, moved to the front of the stage and became a free force. The guitar, bass, and piano had always needed amplification. Now, with combined amplifier modules producing power from 300 to 1500 watts, these formerly unobtrusive instruments became the dominant factors in rock ensembles.

Thus began the age of sound immersion and decibel overkill. And possibly for the first time in the history of music, a musical score included the directions "Build to Chaos." There was little concern for sentimentality as in the superficial and impersonal romantic love songs of the 1950s. The style was direct, uncompromising, and self-sufficient. Still, like all other forms of art expression, rock did not emerge from a complete vacuum, and the musical ingredients of the idiom were shaped by past events. Its style and unique physical presentation burst quite abruptly upon the musical scene. But the sound-terms of the music were an accumulation, or distillation, of techniques from earlier days.

The period of the 1960s has been selected as the principal timespan during which the rock style reached its high point. It is referred to in this text as the "rock period." Although all of the rock reference sources have been drawn from the 1960s, the gestational forces underlying the idiom were clearly apparent in the 1950s and the development of the style has not terminated with the advent of the 1970s.

Harmonic Technique in the Rock Idiom explains the most significant principles underlying the harmony of rock. Its purpose is to provide theoretical understanding and a practical working knowledge of the principal harmonic procedures that characterize the music of the rock idiom.

Part I defines the specific techniques that are applied to the analysis of rock-style illustrations in Part II. The reader should expect a certain amount of duplication in subject headings. Substitute chords, for example, are discussed in both parts. In Part I, the description is explanatory and theoretical; in Part

II, the illustrations are patterned after actual excerpts from rock musical literature.

Part III selectively summarizes the procedures considered most significant in rock chord progressions.

The *Appendix* offers information for historical reference which will interest many readers who wish to study the principal trends in earlier music that formed the basis for developments in twentieth century composition. This concentrated outline of historical precedents traces the chronological development of chord structures and prepares the way for comparison of rock's harmonic procedures with related situations in music of the past.

The Self-Study Workbook supplements the text with programmed instructional drills and applications. The *Workbook* provides learning reinforcement and specific application of the chord patterns summarized in Part III.

Most of the examples from the traditional (non-jazz/rock) literature are shown as harmonic condensations and paraphrases. The original "rock-style" (in the very general sense of the term) illustrations are essentially rhythmicized chord progressions. They are not elaborate because this is not an instrumental or arranging "method book," and the degree of difficulty is geared to an intermediate level.

Readers are expected to choose their own tempos, articulation, and dynamics. Occasional accents and slurs appear in examples when deemed necessary. Compositionally, many musical phrases are not complete. Once the harmonic principle at hand has been made clear, the example is usually terminated. Whole-note harmonic sketches are included for simplified analysis. The voice leading of these sketches is very similar, but not always identical, to that of the more elaborate rhythmicized examples. The harmonic sketches should be played rather slowly, allowing approximately two beats per harmony.

All three-part examples may be played on guitar as well as piano. Pianists will obtain a stronger sense of sonority and definitive progression by doubling the root of each chord with the left hand, or by doubling the entire chord with the left hand an octave below the right hand.

Approximately 600 compositions by leading rock groups and composers of the 1960s have been analyzed for use in this text. More than 200 of these were chosen as reference sources for the various examples of harmonic technique. The given date of any work signifies the first date of known publication, not the date of first performance, recording, or actual composition.

Richard Bobbitt
Boston, Massachusetts

Contents

Part I
Theory; General Definitions and Analytical Procedures

T he harmony of rock is an anachronism.

The theoretical basis of rock chord progression is apparently out of step, in point of time, with its musical surroundings. Rock harmonic practice took formal shape during and after periods of intense harmonic sophistication. Coming, as it did, roughly fifty years after the weighty sonorities of the European impressionists, about thirty years after the principal works of the expressionistic school, and within ten years of the conclusion of the American big band era, the mainstream of rock harmony could well have been expected to provide an innovative and original continuum of structural components. Instead — as sometimes happens with reactionary movements — exactly the opposite occurred.

Harmonically speaking, the rock message is ingenuous and unsophisticated. The chordal vocabulary is uncluttered and unpretentious. The low-tension sonorities are easily identified and hardly innovative. Yet the impact of the harmonic style is singular, quickly recognized, and the contrast with high-tension twentieth century harmonies is obvious and telling. The idiom makes its point by means of harmonic understatement.

The listening ear is pulled backwards in time to the low tension chord structures (triads) of self-taught Renaissance musicians and modally-oriented medievalists. The actual *volume* level of a rock performance is a tympanic assault; but the essence of the *harmonic* material is an echo from the past that persistently demands attention on elemental terms. It turns one on, or it doesn't; there is little room for an equivocal position.

The specific types of rock harmonic devices, however, can not be adequately examined and understood unless one is familiar with the definitions and procedures employed in most of the music common to the harmonic practices of western civilization. Definitions must be generalized and clarified; progressions must be classified; types of chord patterns and chord substitutions must be categorized and the correlation between chordal support and modal alterations understood.

At least one thesis[1] has noted that confusion exists where the nomenclature of harmony is concerned, and it is clear that authors of various "theory" texts are far from unanimous in their acceptance of a particular system. There has been, in fact, no standardization of symbols and numerical nomenclature for the harmonic analysis of music in terms of general techniques acceptable to all theorists. Numerous methods have evolved since the publication of Rameau's *Traité de l'harmonie* (1722) and Fux's *Gradus ad Parnassum* (1725), but no single collection of analytical procedures is completely satisfactory to everyone. It is important, therefore, that particular attention be given to the definitions in this part, in which readers will be made aware of the following:

1. *How to correctly apply proper chord symbols* to progressions that are limited to a single diatonic scale, or to progressions that are non-diatonic (not limited to a single scale).

2. *The commonly used designations* for triads, sevenths, and ninths.

3. *The concept of "master structure"* and non-uniform structures such as triads with added tension tones.

4. How to classify the *four principal types of chord progressions* common to all tonal music.

5. Important *patterns of cadential root motion* and "area prolongation."

6. Chord patterns resulting from the *chord-degree harmonization of melody,* including the six possible triadic harmonizations of a single tone available to rock guitarists.

7. How to use *substitute chords* that provide variations of any rock progression.

8. How to identify *modes, modal interchange, and the blues scale,* including a list of composers and compositions using the blues scale.

A careful study of these definitions and analytical procedures (given in Chapters 1-5) will provide a background for understanding the rock-style musical examples in Part II. The reader is again reminded of the duplication of some subject headings in Part I and Part II. Symmetric harmony, for example, is *theoretically* explained in Part I; in Part II the *application* is shown. The same applies to substitute chords, chord patterns, modal interchange, and other items.

One
Non-Diatonic
Symbolization

Chords restricted to a single scale are traditionally identified by the Roman system of numeration, with or without an indication of the position (inversion) of the chord
by use of a *figured bass*. Given the scale of D minor
(natural), for example, the three-part harmonies of that scale
may be labeled with Roman numerals so as to identify the place
of each chord in the scale.

EX. 1 Scale of D minor (natural)   3p chords with Roman numerals

The exact position, or inversion, of the chord can be indicated by means of additional numbers* that show the type of interval occurring between the lowest tone and each of the tones above it.

EX. 2

In the event, however, that the chord does *not* appear as part of a specific scale, the system of Roman numeration is of little practical use, and other symbolization is needed. The identification of chords by means of letter-names, described below, will also be employed in this study.

3p Chords (Triads)

1. The given letter-name corresponds to the chord root.

2. The type of chord is shown by means of a suffix to the chord letter-name.

   Major: no suffix needed for major
   Minor: m
   Augmented: +
   Diminished: o

---

*In most instances, actual figured bass numbers will not be used for the analysis of progressions that are predominately 3p or 4p upper structures without a separate bass. Only chord symbols and Roman numerals will be used. For example:

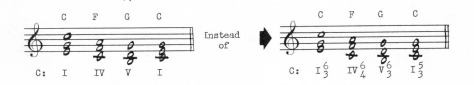

EX. 3 Symbols for triads constructed on the tone F.

Referring again to Ex. 1, letter-name symbols (in addition to the Roman numerals already given) may be shown for each chord:

EX. 4

In non-diatonic situations Roman numerals are considered inappropriate, and only the letter-name with its suffix is used:

EX. 5

4p Chords (Sevenths)

Following are the symbols for commonly used seventh chords constructed on the tone *F*.

EX. 6

5p Chords (Ninths)

Following are the symbols for commonly used ninth chords constructed on the tone *F*.

EX. 7

It has been suggested by Schillinger[2] that the various steps in the development of chord structures are but the realization of successive phases in the utilization of the "master structure" that results from the *expansion* of any seven-unit scale (*e.g.,* major scales, minor scales, or any of the modes). The scale of C Lydian, for example, appears in its non-expanded form as

EX. 8

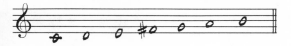

but when expanded, or "opened," it becomes

---

*In all cases, - means *lowered* one half-step, and + means *raised* one half-step.

EX. 9

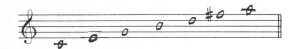

and when arranged vertically, it forms a master structure (MS) that contains all of the substructures inherent to the scale.

EX. 10

Complete MS
for C Lydian →

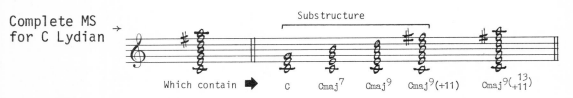

The same scale, of course, can be arranged in its expanded form—expansion zero (E_0)—and also in the second expansion (E_2).

EX. 11

(a) Original scale: C Lydian E_0 (chords in seconds)

(b) Expansion 1 E_1 (chords in thirds, as in Ex. 12)

(c) Expansion 2   E₂ (chords in fourths)

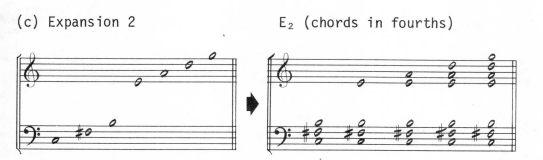

   There are 36 seven-unit scales that have non-identical pitches, and each of these is available as a source of expansion and resultant chord structures. Only a few are shown below, but it should be apparent that even the scales in expansion one provide a varied source of harmonies, since many seven-unit scales have not been customarily used and are still without common names.

EX. 12

(a) C Ionian (major)   MS (E₁)

(b) C Dorian

(c) C Phrygian

(d) C Aeolian (natural minor)

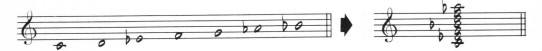

(e) C Harmonic Minor

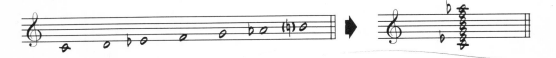

(f) C (no common name)

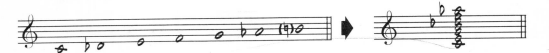

(g) C (no common name)

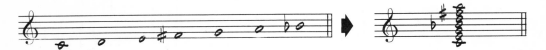

The use of any master structure in its entirety was extremely unusual prior to the twentieth century. The harmonic basis for western music of the Renaissance, Baroque, Classical, and Romantic periods depended upon the substructures of triads, sevenths, and ninths[3]. Elevenths and thirteenths became standard fare around 1900, and the first half of the twentieth century leaned heavily upon ninths, elevenths, and thirteenths as staples of the harmonic vocabulary. Even then, the structures were not always in complete form.

EX. 13   Complete   Incomplete Forms Used in
            Structures   Common Practice

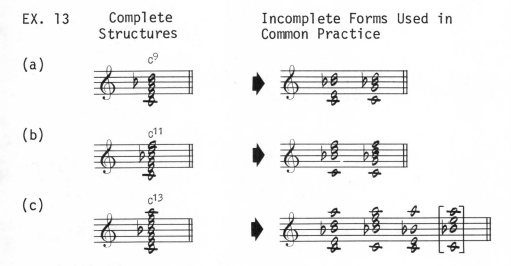

6p and 7p Chords (Elevenths and Thirteenths)

The complete six- and seven-part master structures for eleventh and thirteenth chords are rarely encountered in harmony of the rock period. Symbols for these high-tension harmonies are usually suffixes added to the standard sevenths and ninths of the "dominant" type.

EX. 14

Non-Uniform Structures

The most common structures of the non-uniform type (not in a regular system of thirds) are of the so-called "added sixth" or added ninth variety, and may be either major or minor. The added tones do not normally distort the basic chord quality, since the chord will function independently of the added tone. The principal types (again on the tone *F*) and their symbols[4] are:

EX. 15

Non-uniform structures may also be expanded to include polychords and chords over a pedal point. A horizontal line is used to separate the upper harmonic factor from the lower:

EX. 16

(a) Polychord

(b) Harmony over pedal

In the past, traditional harmonic progressions have often been identified by reference to a particular composition or country. The literature of music history is peppered with terminology that has its nostalgic roots in memories of an outstanding (sometimes innovative) work or composer, or popular usage in some geographical area. This includes expressions such as the "Tristan" chord, the "Scriabin" chord, the "*Lohengrin* Third," the *"Boatmen"* chord of Stravinsky[5], the *"Petrouchka"* or *"Rite of Spring"* chords[6], the French, German, and Italian "sixth" chords and the "Neapolitan Sixth." These early attempts to identify non-diatonic or unconventional structures are inadequate and will be given little consideration, since a practical means of chordal symbolization is presently available. For example, if one wishes to refer to the opening sonorities in the "Prelude" to

Tristan und Isolde[7] it is only necessary to use the specific chord symbols, with enharmonic adjustment where needed.

EX. 17

Likewise, the term "Scriabin" chord provides no information about the harmonic structure. The chord in question can be easily identified and, accordingly, should be.

EX. 18

This study will identify harmonies with Roman numerals as well as with letter names. Choice between the two methods—or the use of both—will be governed entirely by the musical situation. Roman numerals will be limited primarily to diatonic and mixed-diatonic progressions.

Two

The Classification of Harmonic Progressions

The types of chord progressions common to tonal music of western civilization may be generally classified in four categories:

Diatonic: Chord roots and chord structures are restricted to the same scale.

Mixed-Diatonic: Chord roots are restricted to a scale, but chord structures are not restricted to that scale.

Chromatic: Chord structures are derived from linear, half-step connection between parts. Chords are not dependent upon a scale or root pattern.

Symmetric: Chord roots and/or chord structures derive from patterns of intervallic or structural symmetry.

EX. 1 Diatonic Harmony

(a) Scale of C Ionian

(b) Scale of E Dorian

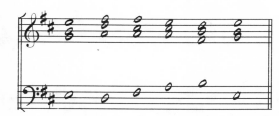

EX. 2 Mixed-Diatonic Harmony

(a) Roots from scale of C
Ionian

(b) Roots from scale of F
Lydian

The choice of chord structures in mixed-diatonic harmony is not limited to major and minor triads, although these are commonly used in rock progressions. Augmented and diminished triads are available, as are sevenths, ninths, elevenths, and thirteenths. The principal requirement of mixed-diatonic harmony is the presence of chord *roots* that are drawn from a specific scale, since such roots permit the progression to retain its quality of modality or diatonicism.

Traditionally, mixed-diatonic harmonies occurred frequently in the form of *secondary dominants* or as alterations of tonic, subdominant, and dominant harmony.

EX. 3

(a) Diatonic progression in   Mixed-diatonic alteration of
    F major   chord structures in original

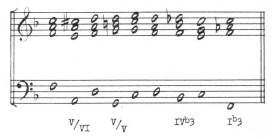

(b) Diatonic progression in   Mixed-diatonic alteration of
    G Aeolian   chord structures in original

EX. 4

(a) J. S. Bach, "Christ lag in Todesbanden," Cantata No. 4

(b) Schumann, <u>Northern Song</u>

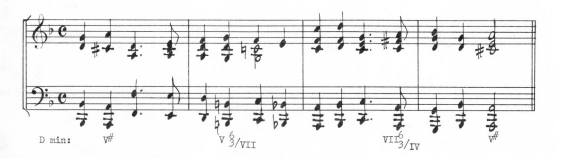

(Roman numerals indicate mixed-diatonic chords: chords
with *roots* in the scale signature, but chord structures not restricted to scale signature.)

Chromatic harmony is most easily recognizable when at
least three tones—*chromatic groups* that form the basis of the
progression—move in half-step motion. The half-step movement
may be up or down.

EX. 5 Chromatic Groups (beginning arbitrarily on the tone <u>G</u>)

The chromatic line may begin on any tone of a chord and,
subsequent to its establishment, other chord tones are added
around the chromatic voice. Each tone of the chromatic group
may be the root, third, fifth, seventh, or higher tension of a
chord.

EX. 6   Chromatic group (beginning arbitrarily with C major chord)

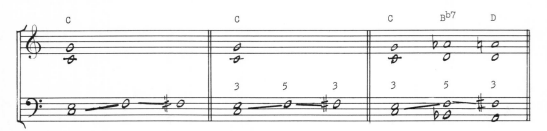

Initial chromatic   Decision concerning   Addition of
gambit   function of each   remaining part
                        chromatic tone

Following is a succession of adjacent chromatic groups. Each group is indicated by lines connecting the tones that move in half-steps.

EX. 7

In the larger sense, the purpose of chromatic harmony is to evoke a response of uncertainty and instability as a contrast to the stable, key-oriented effects of diatonic or mixed-diatonic harmony. Accordingly, the rather aimless quality of the above progression is appropriate to a situation where key stability is not required. Traditionally, however, early usage of chromatic harmony was primarily concerned with the harmonization of chromatic passing tones between diatonic chords.

EX. 8   Some chromatic passing chords (traditional usage)

(a) "French six"   (b) Raised submediant

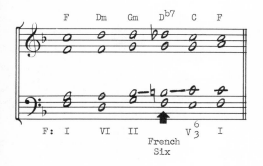

(c) "Neapolitan sixth"

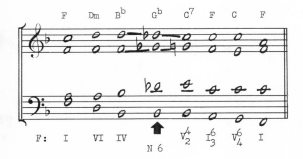

      In some chromatic situations the half-step movement may shift from one part to the other without completion of two consecutive moves in the same part. In all cases the progression should be the result of *linear* half-step motion as opposed to root patterns.

EX. 9

EX. 10 Gesualdo, <u>Moro Lasso</u>
(a) Original

(b) Voice-leading sketch

EX. 11 Wagner, "Prelude," <u>Tristan und Isolde</u>
(a) Reduction and paraphrase

(b) Voice-leading sketch

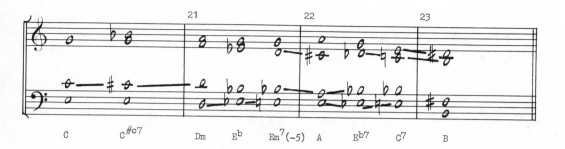

EX. 12   Debussy, <u>Afternoon of a Faun</u>

(a) Reduction and paraphrase

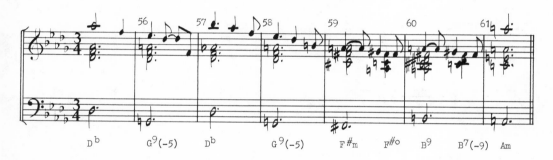

(b) Voice-leading sketch

Reprinted by permission of International Music Company, publisher.

Symmetric harmony normally relies upon intervallic or structural symmetry. *Intervallic symmetry* is most commonly displayed through non-diatonic root progressions. The interval relationships may be uniform or non-uniform and move upward or downward, with or without links.

EX. 13 Symmetric root patterns

(a) Uniform (numbered by half-steps)

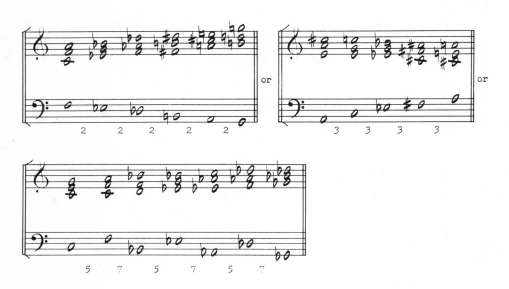

(b) Non-uniform

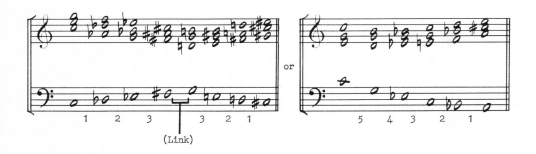

EX. 14 Ravel, <u>String Quartet</u> (Uniform intervallic root-symmetry)

(a) Paraphrase, Movement I

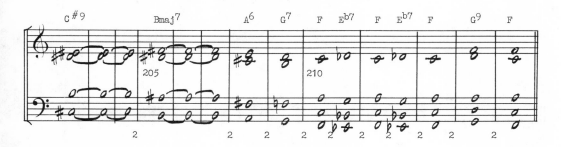

(b) Paraphrase, Movement III, Conclusion

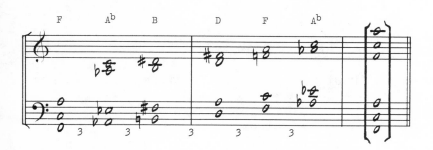

Reprinted by permission of International Music Company, publisher.

      Example 14(b) also illustrates *structural symmetry,* where a fixed pattern of upper structures is maintained—in this case, all major triads. Structural symmetry is not dependent upon root patterns, although it may occur in coincidence with an intervallic root-pattern.

EX. 15   Structural symmetry over symmetric root pattern

Given root progression

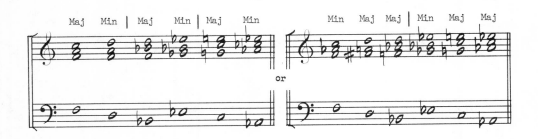

EX. 16   Debussy, <u>Twelve Preludes</u>, Book I, No. 4

Structural symmetry without symmetric root pattern

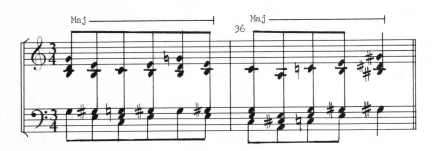

Three
Chord Patterns and Chord-Degree Harmonization

The stylized use of certain diatonic, mixed-diatonic, chromatic, and symmetric chord progressions results in recurring chord patterns that can be classified according to their principal characteristics. The most common patterns of rock harmony fall generally within the following categories:

> Diatonic Root Patterns
>> Chord Structures Diatonic
>> Chord Structures Mixed-Diatonic
> Non-Diatonic Root Patterns
> Chord-Degree Harmonization Patterns

Diatonic root patterns are employed primarily to define harmonic activity into and around the tonic chord of a scale. Important subsidiary chords in a scale, such as the dominant and subdominant harmonies in the conventional major and minor scale, may also be the objective of a root progression. In Examples 1 and 2 the same intervallic root pattern is used to approach the tonic, then the dominant and subdominant:

EX. 1   Diatonic root pattern
        (Roots from F major scale—upper structures diatonic)

(a) Tonic   (b) Dominant   (c) Subdominant
    objective   objective   objective

    I VI II V   I   (I) V III VI II V   (I) IV VI V I IV

EX. 2   Diatonic root pattern
        (Roots from D natural minor scale—upper structures mixed-diatonic)

(a) Tonic   (b) Dominant   (c) Subdominant
    objective   objective   objective

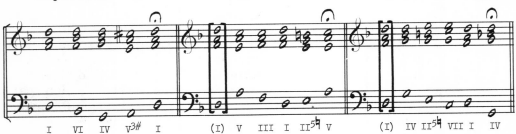

    I VI IV V3# I   (I) V III I II5♮ V   (I) IV II5♮ VII I IV

Non-diatonic root patterns are principally confined to symmetric intervallic motion, frequently in sequence. The common traditional patterns are usually half-step, whole-step, minor third, or cycle of the fifth. The chord structures above the roots, in the rock idiom, are predominantly major or minor triads.

EX. 3   Non-diatonic patterns
        (Roots in intervallic symmetry—upper structures major
        or minor triads)

(a) Whole-steps   (b) Minor thirds

(c) Half-steps   (d) Cycle of the fifth

Some non-diatonic patterns outline, activate, or prolong specific diatonic areas (especially tonic, subdominant, or dominant areas).

EX. 4   Non-diatonic patterns
        (Symmetric sequences prolonging diatonic areas)

(a) Tonic-subdominant prolongation

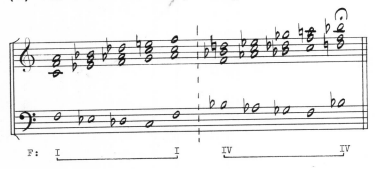

(b) Tonic-dominant minor prolongation

Chord-degree patterns result from the assignment of variable chord-degrees (root, third, or fifth) to the same tone or different tones. The patterns are *harmonization* patterns rather than the realization of root-oriented progressions. The chord degrees of 1 or 3 or 5 are harmonized with either a major or minor triad.

EX. 5

Given tones   Assignment of chord-degrees and harmonization

EX. 6

Sustained tone   Assignment of chord-degrees and harmonization

       The choice of chord-degree and type of chord structure (major or minor) is theoretically arbitrary, and there are no limitations to scale or key; but in practice the technique of chord-degree harmonization tends to generate predictable patterns that operate within key-defined areas. The assignment of chord-degrees may be constant or variable and the order of structures may be constant or variable.

EX. 7

(a) Constant chord-degree, constant structure (major)

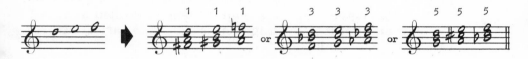

       This type of chord-degree harmonization is the source of the parallel harmonies that are so adaptable to guitar technique. Once the finger positions are set for a particular chord, the same harmony is easily reproduced a whole-step, half-step, or other interval higher or lower by shifting the finger position to a different fret.

(b) Constant chord-degree, variable structure (major-minor-minor)

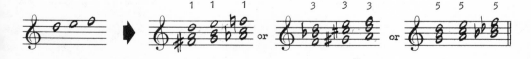

(c) Variable chord-degree, constant structure (minor)

(d) Variable chord-degree, variable structure

It should be apparent that chord-degree harmonization offers a variety of possibilities, even though the tension level is restricted to the root, third, and fifth of major and minor triads. Further, the first and third illustrations in Example 7(d) suggest that the device can be used within key limitations, or as a prolonging mechanism between diatonic chords. Since more than one chord degree can be assigned to a sustained tone, the simplest diatonic melodic fragment is subject to varied interpretation and harmonic variation.

EX. 8   Chord-degree harmonization of five-tone motive from C major scale (Variable chord-degree, constant structure; major)

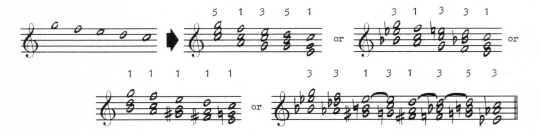

By employing the principles inherent in the above examples, it is possible to generalize a theory of harmonic evolution that provides insight into the sources of chord structures in the tertian system; sources available to the relatively untutored musician and, therefore, easily adopted by rock guitarists. The concepts are as follows:

Concept I: The prevalent chord structures used in rock harmony are the major and/or minor triad. Any melodic tone may be harmonized with a major or minor triad if the given tone is regarded as the root, third, or fifth of the triad. Therefore, any melodic tone may be assigned the chord-degree of 1, 3, or 5.

EX. 9

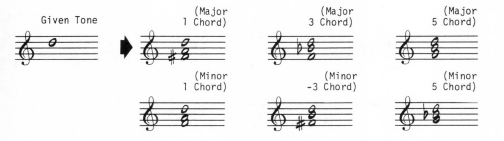

The above example demonstrates that a single melodic tone has six possible harmonizations, even if the chords are limited to major and minor triads.

Concept II: The six available chord-degree harmonizations of a given tone may be applied to separate (repeated) tones or to a sustained tone.

EX. 10

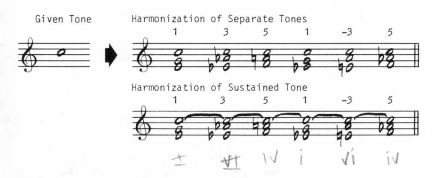

Concept III: The order of appearance of the six available chord-degree harmonizations may be varied. The order of assignment of chord functions is not limited to 1, 3, 5 but may also be 3, 5, 1 or 3, 1, 5 or 1, 5, 3, etc.

EX. 11

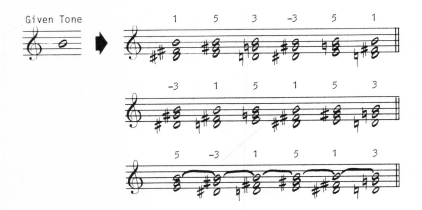

Concept IV: The given melodic tones, to which chord degrees are assigned prior to harmonization, are selected according to their directional tendencies. That is, practical selection of melodic tones to be harmonized will depend upon the manner in which such tones outline, embellish, or approach the root, third, or fifth of the principal chord (or chords) forming the tonal center of a progression.

EX. 12   Tonal center of C major
        Principal chords:

*Dominant major harmony in the rock idiom, as will be noted in Part II, is restricted primarily to V-IV or secondary dominant progressions.

(a) Outlining the tonic (C)

Sustained tones (pedal) of tonic chord

Approaching the root

Approaching the third

Approaching the fifth

(b) Outlining the subdominant (F)

Sustained tones (pedal) of subdominant chord

Approaching the root

Approaching the third

Approaching the fifth

(c) Outlining the dominant

Sustained tones (pedal) of dominant chord

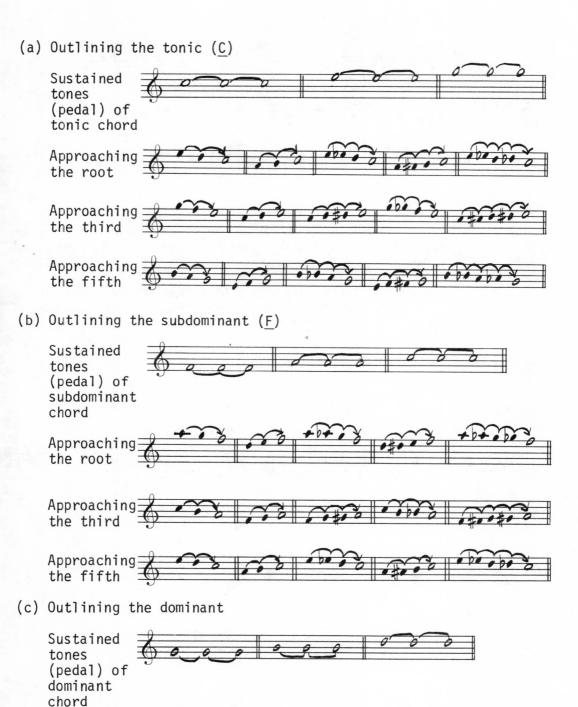

Approaching the root

Approaching the third

Approaching the fifth

Melodic embellishment, as illustrated above, may be applied to the principal chords of any key or temporary tonal center in the same manner.

Concept V: Melodic approach (directional) tones may be repeated, exchanged, or combined prior to assignment of chord degrees.

EX. 13

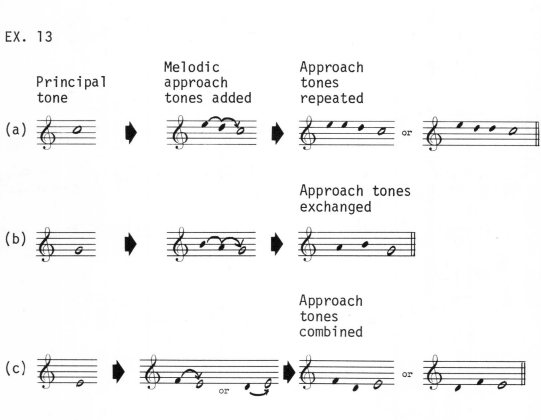

Principal tone

Melodic approach tones added

Approach tones repeated

(a)

or

Approach tones exchanged

(b)

Approach tones combined

(c)

or

or

All of the directional unit patterns evolved through Concepts IV and V immediately become a source of chord-degree harmonization. Chord-degrees may be assigned in constant or variable order and the type of structure may be major or minor in constant or variable combination.

EX. 14

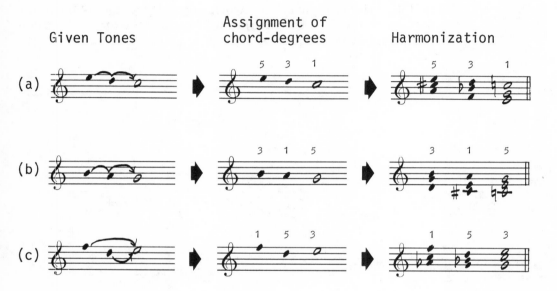

Summary/Addenda

Chord patterns and chord-degree harmonization in rock harmony are principally used to define activity around and into the tonic, subdominant, and dominant (or dominant minor) chords of the key or tonality of the moment. Non-diatonic harmonies occur frequently, but their function is usually to approach and/or complement diatonic chords. Non-diatonic root patterns normally display root motion in half-steps, whole-steps, minor thirds or cycles of the fifth, and between diatonic chords as a device for prolonging or establishing sequences within tonic, subdominant and dominant tonal areas.

Harmonic progressions resulting from the assignment of various chord-degrees (usually 1, 3, or 5) to selected melodic tones of significant duration provide one of the most important sources for the derivation of original harmonies in the rock style.

During the Renaissance, when chord progression was beginning to crystallize into particular patterns of root motion, it was apparent that harmonic progressions were the result of intervallic relationships between melodic lines. The melodies were not simply the activation or ornamentation of preset root patterns. The Renaissance composer did not "realize" a bass line by adding chords, with embellishments, to a given bass part. Root patterns were almost always present—at least through implication—but the motivating forces and principal control factors were melodic. The following two-part framework normally suggests harmonic progression (cycle of the fifth) to well-conditioned twentieth century ears, but the sequence originates in a melodic canon, not a root progression.

EX. 15

In the early Renaissance, the melodic line was the source of chord pattern. During the late Renaissance and Baroque, theories of "fundamental" root progressions gradually evolved (culminating with Rameau's *Traité de l'harmonie* of 1722), and it was common, even in the first quarter of the seventeenth century, to see keyboard parts that provided only a figured bass for the instrumentalist. It was but a short distance from there to the highly organized bass patterns that predominated in theoretical studies of the eighteenth, nineteenth, and early-twentieth centuries.

The return to the melodic tone as a starting point for derivation of harmonic materials occurred (in popular-commercial music) during the period of rock in the 60s. The ever-present guitarist was essentially a melodist; but given a melodic tone, how to find the harmony? The problem was solved by considering each principal melodic tone to be the root, third, or fifth of a major or minor chord, and freedom from pedantically-approved textbook patterns was instantaneous. The result was a varied source of harmonic materials wherein the basic procedures could be generalized in terms of five concepts:

I: Assignment of chord-degrees 1, 3, or 5 to melodic tones.

II: Application of assigned chord-degrees to repeated tones or sustained tones.

III: Variation of the order of assigned chord-degrees.

IV: Selection of melodic tones to be harmonized through consideration of directional tendencies (toward tonal centers) of the tones.

V: Harmonization of repeated, exchanged, or combined directional tones.

Four
Chord Substitutions

An important factor in the development of music in the rock period was the use of various elements that created a sense of ambiguity. Loose song forms, indefinite endings, and jumbled word sequences were deliberately employed in an idiom where, from an establishment point of view, equivocation was the norm. It was to be expected, therefore, that the harmonic techniques of rock would also reflect the overall inclination toward unconventional sound terms. And, indeed, the utilization of chord substitutions proved to be an effective device for the expression of evasive harmonic tendencies.

A *substitute chord,* in this study, is regarded as a chord structure that can take the place of another chord and, accordingly, functionally replace that chord in a given progression.

A triad must have *two common tones* to function as a substitute.

EX. 1

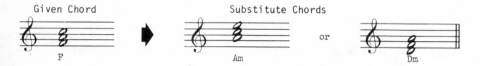

A seventh chord must have *three common tones* to function as a substitute.

EX. 2

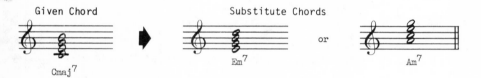

Generally, a substitute chord produces deceptive deviations in a progression or provides an alternative structure that suggests new or additional progressions. The deceptive cadence illustrates one of the earlier uses of substitute chords.

EX. 3

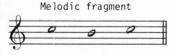

A given melodic fragment (key of C major) may normally be assigned chord-degrees (as described in Chapter 3) and harmonized.

EX. 4

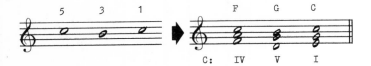

The choice of a different chord-degree for the final chord, however, produces another result.

EX. 5

A similar situation may derive from the plagal cadence.

EX. 6

(a)

Alternate choice:

(b)

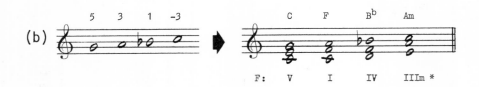

In both instances, the alternate choice of a final chord—generally regarded as a "deceptive" resolution of each harmony—is a substitute chord for the original tonic.

Any substitute chord that has been inserted in a progression also may serve as a new focal point of harmonic activity before the progression returns to its original tonic.

EX. 7

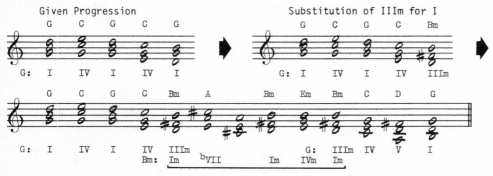

Prolongation of Bm Area

In the song "Eleanor Rigby" (Lennon-McCartney), a single chord and its substitute are alternated throughout the entire composition.

EX. 8

(The same device is used in "You're Lost, Little Girl" by The Doors.)

---

*Redundant identification of minor (versus major) chords may occur frequently in this text. Although it is obvious that the VI chord in C major is a minor chord, the additional use of the "m" suffix obviates any possibility of incorrect identification. This is especially important in dealing with substitute chords, where major and minor structures are constantly being exchanged.

This extremely minimal harmonic activity heightens the sense of ambiguity due to the lack of definitive forward harmonic motion.

A substitute chord, as an alternative structure, also may be treated in the same manner as the original chord for which it is substituted. Since any harmony, in the traditional sense, may be preceded by its secondary dominant, the substitutes for such harmonies can be preceded by secondary dominants:

EX. 9

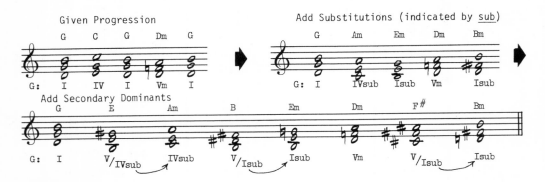

Also, the V (or V₇) of a substitute chord may progress to the *original* chord that the substitute is replacing:

EX. 10

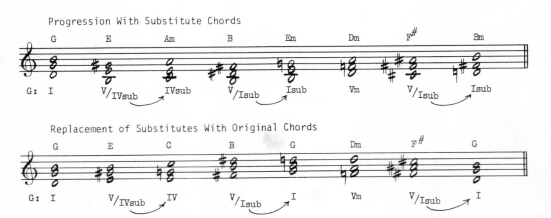

Summary

A basic characteristic of rock harmony is the interchangeability of major and minor chord structures, the roots of such structures being derived from a scale. This, as noted in Chapter 2, is mixed-diatonic harmony, wherein the chord *roots* are restricted to a scale, but the chord *structures* are not; and in spite of the varied structural changes, an essential tonal orientation persists due to the scale-derived roots.

EX. 11

Diatonic progression (G major)

Mixed-diatonic progression (upper structures major or minor, roots from G major scale)

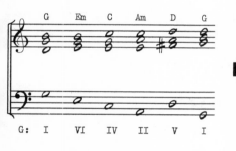

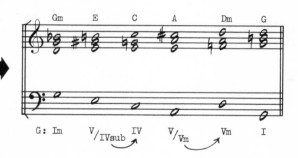

The principles of chord substitution provide the means for controlled variation of mixed-diatonic upper structures. And each substitute chord—*or* the original chord for which it is substituted—may be preceded by a secondary dominant, thus extending and lending further variety to the progression. During the rock period, the principal chords substituted for were the tonic (I or Im), subdominant (IV or IVm) and dominant minor (Vm). Following are the recommended substitutions for each of these harmonies:

EX. 12   Triadic substitutions for I(Im), IV (IVm) and Vm

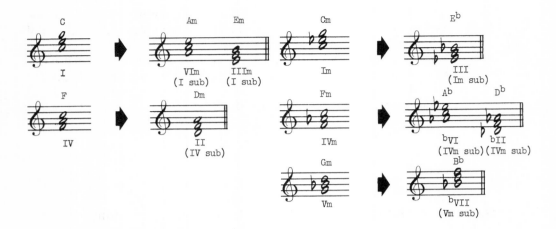

Substitutions for seventh chords (with three tones in common) are handled in similar fashion. Following are the recommended alternatives:

EX. 13

Given chord   Substitutes

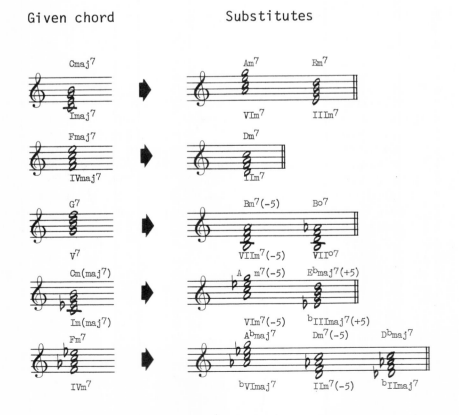

Five
Modes and Modal Interchange

S tudy of the harmonic techniques of the rock period would not be complete without consideration of certain melodic factors that often affected the harmonic continuum: specifically, the melodic-harmonic tendencies that relate to scale-structure and the use of scales to define modality.

A *mode,* in the general sense, is simply a scale. Traditionally, however, the term refers to seven-unit scales whose intervals correspond to those found in the ecclesiastical modes. Since the time of Glareanus (d. 1563), the accepted modes (scales) of the Roman church[8] have formed the basis for the tonal music of western civilization, and they continue to be an important factor in contemporary music.

The following list is not in order of their medieval evolution[9], but it serves the purposes of contemporary usage:

EX. 1   The six standard ecclesiastical modes
(on the root C̲; numbered by half-steps)

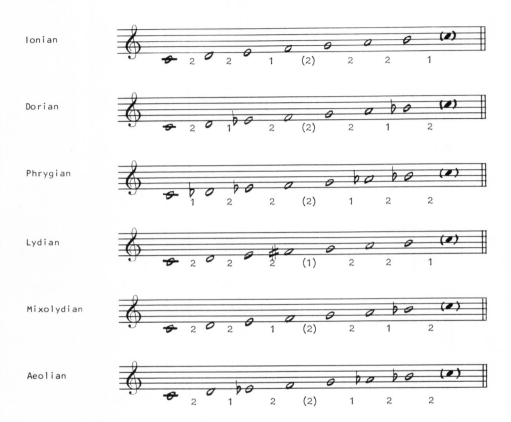

The Locrian mode was not included with the sixteenth-century ecclesiastical modes, apparently due to the tritone interval (and resulting diminished tonic triad) between the root and fifth tone of the scale.

EX. 2

In all cases, the traditional modes corresponded to the intervals of a major scale in root position or displacement. For example, the same interval sequence found in each of the above scales may be obtained by displacing the tones of any major scale, such as the scale of C major:

EX. 3

By definition:

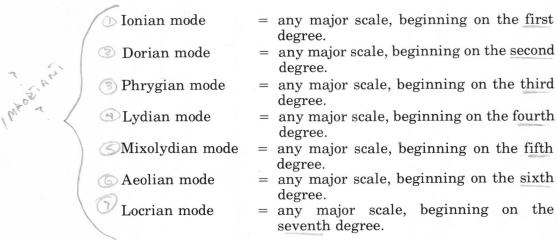

Ⓘ Ionian mode	= any major scale, beginning on the <u>first</u> degree.
Ⓩ Dorian mode	= any major scale, beginning on the <u>second</u> degree.
Ⓩ Phrygian mode	= any major scale, beginning on the <u>third</u> degree.
Ⓩ Lydian mode	= any major scale, beginning on the <u>fourth</u> degree.
Ⓢ Mixolydian mode	= any major scale, beginning on the <u>fifth</u> degree.
Ⓖ Aeolian mode	= any major scale, beginning on the <u>sixth</u> degree.
Ⓖ Locrian mode	= any major scale, beginning on the <u>seventh</u> degree.

Thus the following melody with key signature of *two sharps* and principal *melodic axis* (tone center) on *A* is in the Mixolydian (fifth degree) mode:

EX. 4

Likewise, the next melody with key signature of *one flat* and principal melodic axis on *G* is in the Dorian (second degree) mode:

EX. 5

A *modal modulation* signifies the establishment of a new scale. The new scale may relate to the same tone axis or a different tone axis:

EX. 6

Sometimes a temporary interchange takes place between two different modes. In such cases, the sudden switch to another mode, and back again, is not of sufficient time duration to effect a modulation. The situation, known as *modal interchange* results from the alternation between a tone of an established scale and its own chromatic modification. The interchange may occur in a linear (single-line melody) or vertical (superposed) setting.

EX. 7   Juxtaposed modal interchange
         (interchange of lowered third and natural third)

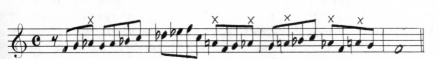

EX. 8   Superimposed modal interchange
         (interchange of B-flat and B-natural.
         F major over F Lydian)

The effect of modal interchange upon harmonic structure becomes more apparent when the altered chromatic tone is superposed directly against a tone of the same letter name in the same chord. A lowered seventh, for example, against a natural seventh; or a lowered third against a natural third, as in the following:

EX. 9 Superposed modal interchange

Individual chords may also be juxtaposed against their own chromatic modification. This is *chordal modal interchange* (much used in rock progressions) and usually involves the alternation or exchange of I major-I minor, or IV major-IV minor, or V major-V minor. It was quite ordinary in Renaissance, Baroque, and early Classical period compositions to end works in a *minor* tonality with a *major* chord. The change of the minor third of the tonic chord to a major third is termed "Picardy third" *(tierce de Picardie)*.

The following traditional excerpts contain several instances of chordal modal interchange.

EX. 10   Monteverdi, "Lament" (from the opera <u>Arianna</u>, 1608)

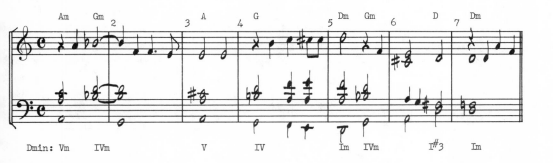

The Vm (Am) interchanges with the V major (A): m.1, 3.
The IVm (Gm) interchanges with the IV major (G): m.1, 4, 5.
The Im (Dm) interchanges with the I major (D): m.5, 6, 7.

EX. 11   Orlando di Lasso (d. 1594), <u>Tristis est Anima Mea</u> (motet)

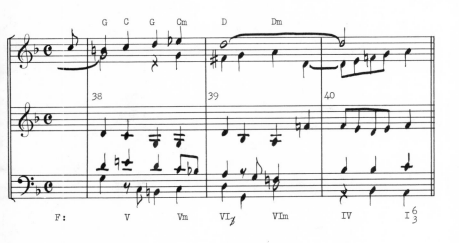

The V major (C) interchanges with the Vm (Cm): m.38.
The VI major (D) interchanges with the VIm (Dm): m.39.

EX. 12 Caccini (d. 1618) <u>Dovro dunque morire</u> (madrigal)

The Im (Gm) interchanges with the I major (G): m.1, 2, 6.
The V major (D) interchanges with the V minor (Dm): m.4, 5, 6, 7.

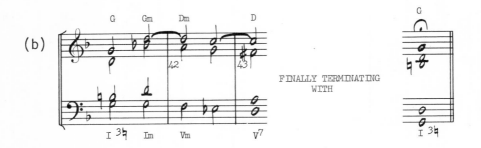

FINALLY TERMINATING
WITH

The I major (G) interchanges with the I minor (Gm): m.41 and final chord.
The V minor (Dm) interchanges with the V major (D): m.42, 43.

The final chord provides the typical ending of the Picardy third. The one flat of the key signature is in keeping with the overall modal ambiguity, since it gives no definite information regarding the specific modality of the piece. The similarity between the modal ambiguities of the Renaissance (and early Baroque) and the rock period is striking. Often, in any art medium, the processes of evolution (at certain stages) are not unlike the processes of dissolution. The sculpture of primitive peoples, for example, frequently resembles the sculpture of modern artists who make a conscious effort to eliminate excess adornment and reduce their configurations to bare essentials.

   The *Gymnopédies* (1888) for piano of Erik Satie are interesting examples of ambiguous modal treatment from the past. It is not surprising that these ingenuous pieces continue to appeal to musicians of our day, including rock musicians[10], since ambiguity, equivocal chordal progression, substitute chords, and modal vacillation play an important part in the rock harmonic idiom.

EX. 13   Satie, <u>Gymnopédie No. 1</u> (1888)

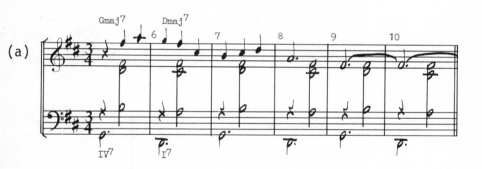

The above passage, completely diatonic to D Ionian, soon shifts to D Dorian:

Used by permission of G. Schirmer, Inc.

and the modal transitions between Ionian and Dorian continue throughout. The Vm of the final cadence later becomes a typical device in the rock period for avoiding the usual dominant-tonic authentic cadence:

(c)

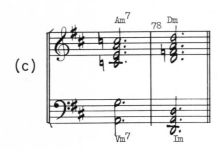

The Blues Scale

Although the major-minor scales and ecclesiastical modes provide the melodic material for most traditional western music, many other scales are obviously available. These may range in structure from three to twelve units and include popular cliché scales such as the whole-step and pentatonic:

EX. 14

(a) Pentatonic major   (b) Pentatonic minor   (c) Whole-Step scale
    on C   on C   on C

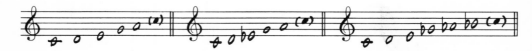

In rock (and jazz/rock), however, a more frequently used scale is the *blues scale,* which (when compared to the major scale) has lowered third, lowered fifth, and lowered seventh degree interpolations.

EX. 15   C major scale with "blue note" interpolations

As long as the lowered third, lowered fifth, and lowered seventh of this scale are used, it is not necessary to include all of the other tones.

EX. 16

In fact, some writers restrict the structure of the blues scale to six tones.[11]

EX. 17

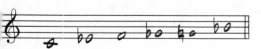

In any case, it is important to realize that, in rock, the three blue notes are frequently used against a *major* chord.

EX. 18

Summary/Addenda

The analytical procedures necessary for descriptive examination of rock harmonic technique have concentrated, in Part I, on chord structure and chord progression as such. Symbolization, progression classification, root patterns, basic concepts of harmonization, and substitute chords have been the principal objects of definition and analysis.

Items relating to melodic analysis, such as scales and modes, were also included because there are some situations in which harmonic-melodic interaction is significant, and it is also important to have at hand adequate terminology when the need arises.

Because this text is not a study of melodic technique, there is no attention to melodic analysis in Part II. Therefore, reference sources* illustrating the use of modal influences and/or blues scales are included here rather than in Part II. The particular device referred to is indicated with each group of sources.

---

*References to specific rock compositions will be by title and composer's name. The performing group (Bee Gees, etc.) by whom the composer was featured can be identified by referring to the *Bibliography*. Only The Doors do not provide the names of individual composers.

Source References

Modal Interchange

"After Midnight"
(J. Cale), m.1-11

(chordal interchange, I major-I minor)

"Green River"
(J. Fogerty), m.1-5

(superposed interchange, lowered third-natural third)

"I Can See for Miles"
(P. Townsend), m.1-5 17-21

(chordal interchange, I major-I minor)

"Satisfaction"
(Jagger-Richards), m.3-9

(juxtaposed interchange, natural fifth-lowered fifth)

Blues Scale

Composition	Measure	Blue Notes (lowered)	Supporting Harmony
"Blue Jay Way" (G. Harrison)	Throughout	3, 5	I
"Green River" (J. Fogerty)	Throughout	3, 7	I
"I Feel Fine" (Lennon-McCartney)	1-3	7	I
"I'll Go Crazy" (J. Brown)	Throughout	3, 5	I
"I'm Losing You" (Grant-Whitfield-Holland)	Throughout	3, 7	I
"Knocking Around the Zoo" (J. Taylor)	47-50	7	I
"Mama Gets High" (Bargeron-Katz)	1-4	3, 7	I
"Night Owl" (J. Taylor)	1-3	3, 7	I
"Sinister Purpose" (J. Fogerty)	1-4	3, 7	I
"How Can I Be Sure" (Cavaliere-Brigati)	7-15	7	Im or Im (sub)
"I Can See for Miles" (P. Townsend)	1-3	3	Im or Im (sub)
Jesus Christ, Superstar, IX (Rice-Webber)	1-2	3, 7	Im or Im (sub)
"Satisfaction" (Jagger-Richards)	1-13	3, 7	Im or Im (sub)
"Chameleon" (J. Fogerty)	1-3	3	IV
"Country Girl" (N. Young)	72-20	3	IV
"Hawg for You" (O. Redding)	5-7	3, 7	IV
"Sinister Purpose" (J. Fogerty)	9-12	3	IV
"Stamped Ideas" (Ingle-Deloach)	1-3	3	IV
"Fifty-first Anniversary" (J. Hendrix)	1-5	7	V or Vm
"Hawg for You" (O. Redding)	9-11; 21-23	3, 7	V or Vm
"Papa's Got a Brand New Bag" (J. Brown)	9; 21	3	V or Vm
"Never Can Say Goodbye" (C. Davis)	1-6	7	V or Vm

Part II

Source References from Selected Rock Compositions; Illustrations of Principal Harmonic Techniques

Part II

Source References from Selected Rock Compositions; Illustrations of Principal Harmonic Techniques

The analysis of rock compositions in this text has been confined to works by principal groups that originated and/or markedly influenced the music of the rock period. Stylistic divisions are, of course, controversial, and no agreement has been reached by musicians as to the exact meaning of certain designations commonly applied to various style characteristics. Categorization of the groups below, however, should be adequate for most readers. No ranking or implied order of importance is intended.

Since, due to copyright restrictions, it is not possible to quote directly from published rock compositions, all of the examples in this part have been composed to illustrate particular harmonic techniques. Rock source material references are given after the examples.

1. *English Rock*

   The Beatles
   Bee Gees
     (Australian; tendency
     toward soft rock; use of
     strings)
   The Rolling Stones
     (Tendency toward hard
     rock)
   The Who

2. *Hard/Acid Rock*

   (Unrestrained, high-
   decibel, abrasive; includes
   psychedelic media devices
   and props)

   Cream
   The Doors
   Iron Butterfly
   Jefferson Airplane
   Jimi Hendrix (Soloist)
   The Rascals

3. *Soul*

   (Updated, black, rhythm
   and blues, but with strong
   gospel influence. Emphasis
   on phrasic ostinato, or
   "riffs")

   James Brown (Soloist)
   Otis Redding (Soloist)
   Sly and the Family Stone
   Supremes (Diana Ross,
   Soloist)

4. *Rock-Jazz*

   (Amalgamation of rock
   beat with jazz melodic-
   harmonic influences)

   Blood, Sweat and Tears
     (Also uses brass and
     woodwinds)
   Chicago

5. *Soft Rock*

   (Smooth, nonabrasive)

   The Association
   The Carpenters
   The 5th Dimension

6. *Latin Rock*

   Brasil 66
     (Soft rock tendency)
   Santana

7. *Folk Rock*

   (Poetic, with a "message;"
   strongly influenced by Bob
   Dylan and country-
   western)

   Creedence Clearwater
   Crosby, Stills, Nash, and
   Young
   James Taylor (Soloist)
   Seals and Croft
   Simon and Garfunkel

8. *Burt Bacharach/Jimmy
   Webb*

   (Most significant "standard
   tune" composers of 60s. Not
   specifically rock composers,
   but strongly influenced by
   the rock movement; their
   music featured by soft rock
   groups)

Six

The Cadential Dominant
Minor; Symmetric Patterns

C adences, in this text, are more than a means of attaining "momentary or permanent conclusion."[1] Here they are regarded as chord progressions that delineate, and point toward, a tonal center or "tonic-like" area; the cadential thrust may outline a temporary tonal center as well as a more permanent one.

In the rock idiom, there are a few outstanding principles to be observed regarding cadential treatment:

1. Avoid the V-I or IV-V-I authentic cadence (unless intentionally duplicating traditional harmonic practices).

2. Use the dominant major chord only
    a. as a *secondary dominant,* or
    b. to *precede* the IV chord (see Chapter 7),
    c. in the *deceptive cadence* (see Chapter 8).

Exceptions to the above, of course, will be discovered by the student. But the unique quality of the more effective and characteristic rock progressions is due, in large measure, to avoidance of the V-I or IV-V-I cadence. Remember that deliberate ambiguity is an important feature of the rock philosophy.

The *dominant minor* provides a favored alternative to the usual V-I progression. Although it has become a cliche in the rock idiom, it appears only sporadically in traditional music. The following example is quoted from a late nineteenth century harmonization by Thomas Helmore (d. 1890) of a ninth century Latin hymn:

EX. 1   <u>Veni Emmanuel</u> (closing measures)

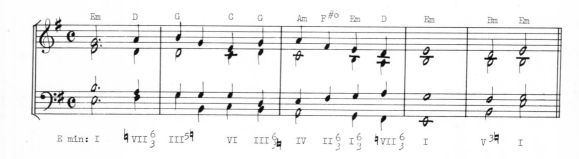

In modern usage, cadences employing the Vm are usually as follows:

EX. 2

(a) Vm-I

(b) Vm-Im

(c) Vm(sub)-I

(d) Vm(sub)-Im

The Vm also occurs frequently in combination with the IV chord, but progressions in that category will be given in the next chapter. A few examples of the Vm(sub) are included in this chapter, however, since it is an important feature of the Vm-type cadence. Substitute chords in general are examined in Chapter 8.

EX. 3   Vm-I

Harmonic sketch

Source References

"Forty Thousand Headmen" (Winwood-Capaldi), m.1-12
"I Wanna Be Your Man" (Lennon-McCartney), m.8-12
"I'm Sick Y'all" (Redding-Cropper-Porter), throughout
"Moon Turn the Tides" (J. Hendrix), throughout

EX. 4 Vm-Im

Harmonic sketch

Source References

"Everything's All Right" from *Jesus Christ Superstar* (Rice-Webber), m.11-13
"Summer's Almost Gone" (The Doors), m.1-4; second ending
"Things We Said Today" (Lennon-McCartney), m.1-16

There are also occasional instances where the dominant minor in the Vm-Im progression occurs as a seventh chord (minor seventh).

EX. 5   Vm7-Im

Source References

"Black Magic Woman" (P. Green), m.1-10
"Fire and Rain" (J. Taylor), m.1-4
"Things We Said Today" (Lennon-McCartney), m.1-6

EX. 6   Vm(sub)-I, or Im

Source References

"Kilburn Towers" (Gibb-Gibb), throughout
"Masters of War" (B. Dylan), throughout
"Most Anything You Want" (D. Ingle), throughout
"Up From the Skies" (J. Hendrix), m.43-62

Symmetric patterns in rock music are usually of the root progression type, wherein non-diatonic root patterns outline symmetric intervallic root motion in half-steps, whole-steps, minor thirds, or cycle of the fifth. In most cases the tendency is to concentrate upon short patterns of whole-step symmetry that point toward the tonic or dominant chords of the tonality of the moment. Other common uses of symmetry in rock include symmetric sequences and symmetric "prolongations."

EX. 7 Symmetric whole-step roots (into the tonic)

(a)

Harmonic sketch

(b)

Harmonic sketch

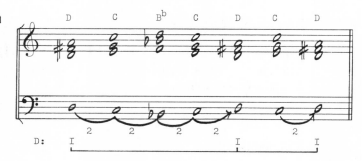

Source References

"All Along the Watchtower" (B. Dylan), m.1-4
"Beginnings" (R. Lamm), m.115-123
"California Dreaming" (J. Phillips), m.32-36
"Kozmic Blues" (Joplin-Mekler), m.8-13
"Stand" (S. Stewart), *Coda*
"To Be Free" (J. Pankow), m.1-9
"Up, Up and Away" (J. Webb), first, second and third endings
"Whiskey Man" (J. Entwhistle), m.1-4
"Wichita Lineman" (J. Webb), *coda*

EX. 8   Symmetric whole-step roots (into the dominant)

Harmonic sketch

Source References

"The Ballad of You and Me and Pooneil" (P. Kantner), m.17-25
"The Battle" (Katz-Halligan), m.9-10; 23-24
"1983" (J. Hendrix), m.1-6

EX. 9   Symmetric Sequence

Harmonic sketch

Original pattern   Pattern repeats minor
in whole-steps   third above starting tone

Source References

"In the Country" (T. Kath), m.17-18
"In-A-Gadda-Da-Vida" (D. Ingle), m.11-19
"Love Street" (The Doors), m.9-16
"Orange Air" (J. Webb), m.17-28
"Stand" (S. Stewart), m.1-9
"Something" (G. Harrison), m.1-6

Symmetric patterns are also employed in the extension or prolongation of harmonic areas, the latter usually being confined to the tonic, subdominant, or dominant.

The concept of *area prolongation* appears to have been introduced by Heinrich Schenker[2], a nineteenth century theorist who suggested that the majority of chord progressions in Baroque, Classical, and Romantic period music were the result of a "filling-in" or prolongation of the harmonic areas of the tonic, dominant, or subdominant. The principle of prolongation has been expanded in twentieth century practice and broader versions of the theory are in common use.

For example, one may activate, fill-in, or prolong the harmonic area of a single chord, or the area between any two chords (such as tonic-dominant or tonic-subdominant) by introducing additional tones that may be used as a source of new harmonies. The added tones may be in the melody or in the bass, and are subject to chord-degree harmonization. This is simply a restriction of the chord-degree harmonization technique (Part I, Chapter 3) to a specific harmonic area.

EX. 10

(a) Prolongation of tonic area (melodically derived)

Approach (fill-in) tones added

Assign chord-degrees   **Harmonization**

(b) Prolongation of tonic-subdominant minor area (melodically derived)

Approach (fill-in) tones added

Assign chord-degrees   **Harmonization**

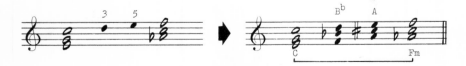

(c) Prolongation of the dominant-tonic area
   (derived from added roots)

**Fill-in tones added
(all roots)**

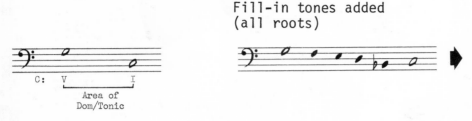

C: V   I
⌊_____⌋
Area of
Dom/Tonic

Harmonization

Most chord-degree harmonizations are applied to melodic situations. But there are many area prolongations in rock that activate and extend a given harmonic area through the process of filling in new root progressions between principal chords of the key. Such prolongations are often symmetrically controlled.

EX. 11   Symmetric prolongation of the dominant area

Whole-Step Roots, Constant Structure

Whole-step roots, constant structure

EX. 12 Symmetric prolongation of the subdominant area

Harmonic sketch

Whole-step roots, constant structure.
In this case, the F♯ and E harmonies are also
preceded by secondary subdominants.

EX. 13 Symmetric prolongation of the tonic area

Harmonic sketch

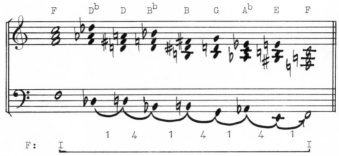

Symmetric roots in major thirds and
half-steps.   Constant structure.

Source References

"Come On Up" (F. Cavaliere), m.1-7 (tonic prolongation)
"Idea" (Gibb-Gibb), m.8-21 (subdominant prolongation)
"It's Just a Thought" (J. Fogerty), m.28-30 (subdominant pro-
longation)
"Little Miss Strange" (N. Redding), m.8-14 (dominant prolonga-
tion)
"Tribute to a King" (Bell-Jones), m.1-5 (dominant prolongation)

Summary/Addenda

The use of the cadential dominant minor and certain
symmetric patterns in place of conventional cadence progressions points out rock's tendency to stress ambiguity and uncertainty. This tendency is carried to further extremes in situations where definitive resolution into the tonic of the moment is
specifically avoided (see Chapter 8).

Although the popularity of the conventional dominant
major chord has yielded to widespread use of the dominant
minor, the former *is* used as a secondary dominant, in deceptive
cadences (especially V-VI) and to precede the subdominant in
V-IV progressions (see next chapter). Sometimes the dominant
major appears in conjunction with the dominant minor (or its
substitute) in chordal modal interchange (Part I, Chapter 5),
where a major chord alternates with a minor chord on the same
root.

EX. 14

(a)

V major (C) interchanges with the Vm (Cm)

(b)

V major (C) interchanges with the Vm(sub) (E♭)

Source References

"Fire and Rain" (J. Taylor), m.1-5
"Let There Be Love" (Gibb-Gibb), introduction
"Takin' It In" (J Taylor), m.2-7
"You Don't Have to Cry" (S. Stills), m.1-17
"You Keep Me Hangin' On" (Holland-Dozier), m.21-23; 71-73

Alternation or exchange between the V and Vm (or its substitute) in chordal modal interchange is often extended to include temporary tonal centers other than the tonic. For example, the concept is sometimes applied to the dominant area.

EX. 15

Harmonic sketch

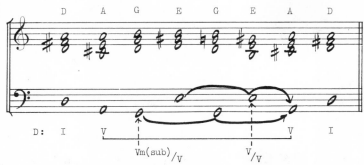

Here, the exchange between the Vm(sub) of V and the V major of V provides a prolongation of the dominant area.

Source Reference

"The Big Bright Green Pleasure Machine" (P. Simon), m.67-73

Seven
Subdominant Harmony

The tendency to avoid conventional dominant-tonic relationships in rock music has led to emphasis on subdominant harmony, including both the subdominant major and minor.

The subdominant cadences most common in compositions of the rock period include

IV-I	V-IV-I
IVm-I	Vm-IV-I
IV-Im	Vm(sub)-IV-I
IVm-Im	

The following nine examples illustrate, in turn, each of the above patterns.

EX. 1 IV-I

Harmonic sketch

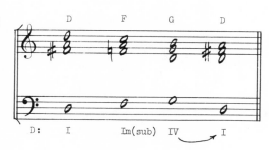

Source References

"After Midnight" (J. Cale), m.1-5

"All Things Must Pass" (G. Harrison), throughout

"Does Anybody Really Know What Time It is (R. Lamm), throughout

"Hey Jude" (Lennon-McCartney), throughout

"I Can See for Miles" (P. Townsend), throughout

"In the Midnight Hour" (Pickett-Cropper), throughout

"It's Just a Thought" (J. Fogerty), throughout

"I've Told You for the Last Time" (Cropper-Bramlett), through-out

"Magic Garden" (J. Webb), m.41-52

"Movin' In" (J. Pankow), throughout

"Satisfaction" (Jagger-Richard), throughout

"She Said She Said" (Lennon-McCartney), throughout

"We've Only Just Begun" (Williams-Nichols), m.19-22

"Whiskey Man" (J. Entwhistle), m.8-15

"Who'll Stop the Rain" (J. Fogerty), throughout

"Yellow Submarine" (Lennon-McCartney), throughout

"Yesterday" (Lennon-McCartny), m.7; 14

EX. 2 IVm-I

Harmonic sketch

Source References

"How Can I Be Sure" (Cavaliere-Brigati), first ending
"If I Fell" (Lennon-McCartney), m.34-38
"I'm On a Trip to Your Heart" (S. Stewart), m.2-9
"Nowhere Man" (Lennon-McCartney), final cadence
"Tales of Brave Ulysses" (Clapton-Sharp), throughout
"The Look of Love" (David-Bacharach), m.6-14

EX. 3 IV-Im

Harmonic sketch

Source References

"Helplessly Hoping" (S. Stills), m.1-9
"Come Together" (Lennon-McCartney), m.7-10
"Country Girl" (N. Young), throughout
"Cut My Hair" (D. Crosby), throughout
"Oye Como Va" (T. Puente), throughout
"Moon Turn the Tides" (J. Hendrix), m.10-17

EX. 4   IVm-IM

Harmonic sketch

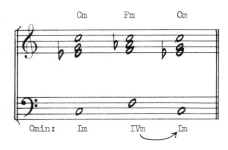

Source References

"Black Magic Woman" (P. Green), throughout
"In the Time of Our Lives" (Ingle-Bushy), m.1-11; 31-37
"Kozmic Blues" (Joplin-Mekler), throughout
"Little Wing" (J. Hendrix), throughout
"Strange Days" (The Doors), m.5-11
"Summer's Almost Gone" (The Doors), m.4-7; 23-27; final cadence

EX. 5   V-IV-I

(a)

Harmonic sketch

(b)

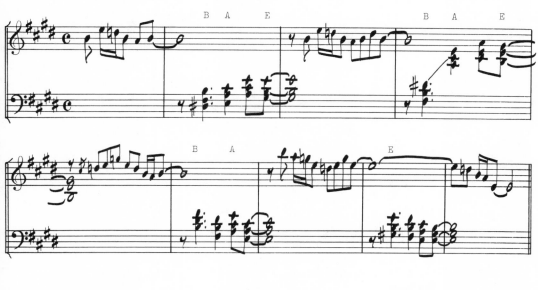

Harmonic sketch

(c)

Harmonic sketch

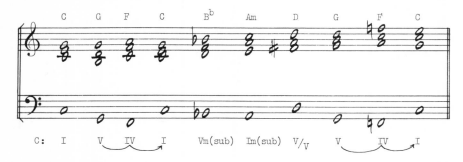

Source References

"Bad Moon Rising" (J. Fogerty), m.1-4
"Chameleon" (J. Fogerty), throughout
"Helpless" (N. Young), m.1-4
"Fifty-first Anniversary" (J. Hendrix), m.1-4
"Indian Gin and Whiskey Dry" (Gibb-Gibb), throughout
"One Rainy Wish" (J. Hendrix), m.20-24
"Please Go Home" (Jagger-Richard), m.1-7
"Yellow Submarine" (Lennon-McCartney), m.1-6

EX. 6 Vm-IV-I

Harmonic sketch

Source References

"All Things Must Pass" (G. Harrison), m.9-11; second ending
"I Can't See Nobody" (Gibb-Gibb), m.9-15
"Let It Rain" (Bramlett-Clapton), m.1-8
"She Said She Said" (Lennon-McCartney), m.1-5

EX. 7   Vm(sub)-IV-I

Harmonic sketch

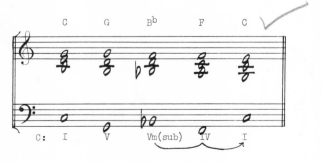

It should be noted that the Vm(sub)-IV relationship is actually the latter part of the so-called "secondary subdominant chain."

The common symmetrical pattern known as the "cycle of the fifth" has its reflection in the symmetrical cyclic pattern of the "negative fifth"[3], where the basic root motion is *up* a perfect fifth rather than *down* a perfect fifth.

For example, the tonic root *C* may be approached by the tone a perfect fifth above:

EX. 8

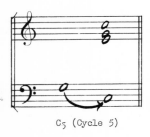

C₅ (Cycle 5)

or by the tone a perfect fifth below:

EX. 9

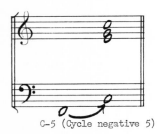

C-5 (Cycle negative 5)

Either of these moves may be extended to form a complete cyclic pattern:

EX. 10

(a) Continuous cycle 5

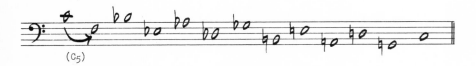

(C₅)

(b) Continuous cycle negative 5

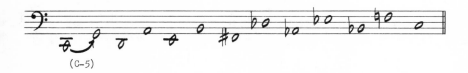

(C–5)

The last three roots in Example 10(b) conform to progression Vm(sub)-V-I:

EX. 11

C: Vm(sub)   IV   I

If additional roots are utilized from 10(b), a series of chords results that forms a chain of secondary subdominants. Following are the last six roots with upper structures (major) added:

EX. 12   Secondary subdominants

The final example illustrating the Vm(sub)-IV-I progression contains secondary subdominants:

EX. 13

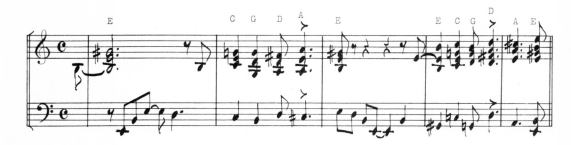

Harmonic sketch

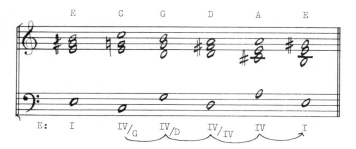

In accord with the system of analysis used in this study, however, the same progression should be symbolized in terms of the *substitute function* of each harmony:

EX. 14

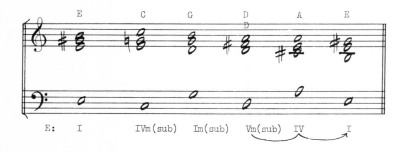

Source References

"Don't Know Why" (Bramlett-Clapton), introduction; *coda*
"Helplessly Hoping" (S. Stills), throughout
"Here Comes the Sun" (G. Harrison), m.47-53
"Hey Jude" (Lennon-McCartney), m.73-76
"Hideway" (J. Fogerty), m.1-4
"Lady Jane" (Jagger-Richard), m.2-10
"Never My Love" (D. Addrisi), m.1-4
"1983" (J. Hendrix), m.23-45
"Please Go Home" (Jagger-Richard), throughout
"She Said She Said" (Lennon-McCartney), m.1-10
"Summer Breeze" (Seals-Croft), m.1-6
"You Don't Have to Cry" (S. Stills), m.1-11

Eight

Substitute Chords

Substitute chords, as used in rock compositions, are found primarily in cadential tonic (or "tonality of the moment") situations—including deceptive cadences—and area prolongations. Since chord substitution is one of the most important features of rock harmonic teachnique, Part I, Chapter 4 should be reviewed before analyzing the illustrations in this chapter.

The principal categories for the use of substitute chords (all examples in tonal area of C) are:

A. Substitutions for the tonic (I) and tonic minor (Im),

EX. 1

Substitutions

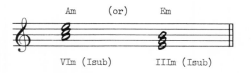

Substitution

Im (Tonic Minor)

^{b}III (Im sub)

B. Substitutions for the subdominant (IV) and subdominant minor (IVm),

EX. 2

Substitutions

IV (Subdom. Major)

IIm (IVsub)

IVm (Subdom. Minor)

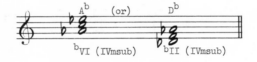

^{b}VI (IVmsub) ^{b}II (IVmsub)

C. Substitution for the dominant minor (Vm),

EX. 3

Substitution

Vm (Dom. Minor)

^{b}VII (Vmsub)

D. Area prolongations of the tonic,

E. Deceptive cadences, including the so-called *"fade coda."*

The following examples and source references illustrate the five categories of chord substitution:

Substitution for the Tonic

EX. 4

Harmonic sketch

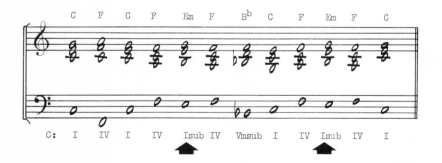

EX. 5

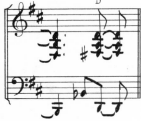

Harmonic sketch

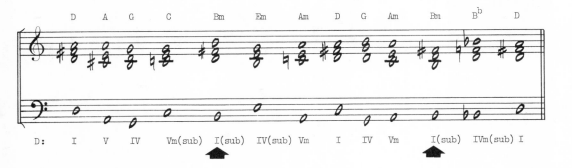

Source References

"Chameleon" (J. Fogerty), m.1-4
"Child of Clay" (Maresca-Curtis), m.1-5
"Eleanor Rigby" (Lennon-McCartney), m.1-16
"Get Ready" (W. Robinson), m.1-3
"Let Me Go To Him" (David-Bacharach), m.21-29 (compare with
    "What the World Needs Now")
"Run of the Mill' (G. Harrison), m.1-5

"What the World Needs Now" (David-Bacharach), m.1-4 (compare with "Let Me Go To Him")
"You're Lost Little Girl" (The Doors), m.1-10

Substitution for the Tonic Minor

EX. 6

Harmonic sketch

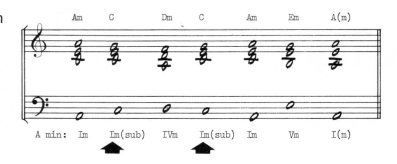

*third omitted, but modality implied by preceding events.

EX. 7

Harmonic sketch

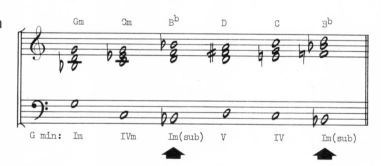

Source References

"After Midnight" (J. Cale), m.1-4
"I'm Losing You" (Grant-Whitfield-Holland), m.1-5
"More Than Words Can Say" (Floyd-Jones), m.9-20
"Steppin' Stone" (Boyce-Hart), m.9-14

Substitution for the Subdominant

EX. 8

Harmonic sketch

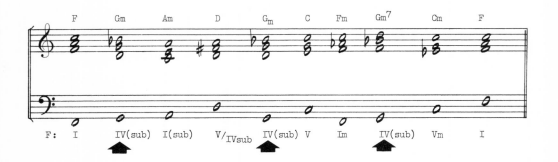

Source References

"Everything Is Good About You" (Holland-Dean), m.1-4; 26-29
"Let It Rain" (Bramlett-Clapton), m.45-50
"Summer's Daughter" (J. Webb), m.45-51

Substitutions for the Subdominant Minor

EX. 9

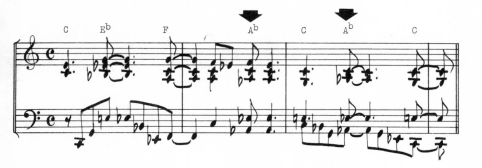

Harmonic sketch

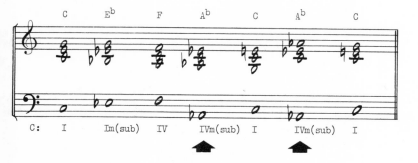

EX. 10

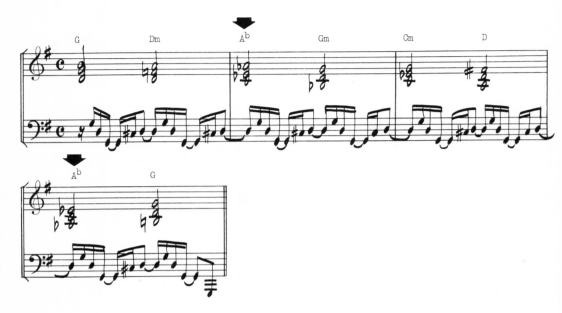

Harmonic sketch

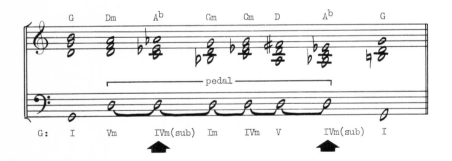

Source References

"A Hazy Shade of Winter" (P. Simon), m.1-11
"I, Me, Mine" (G. Harrison), m.31-39
"My World Is Empty without You" (Holland-Dozier), m.1-8; *coda*
"Stamped Ideas" (Ingle-DeLoach), throughout
"Steppin' Stone" (Boyce-Hart), throughout
"Tales of Brave Ulysses" (Clapton-Sharp), m.5-9

Substitution for the Dominant Minor

EX. 11

Harmonic sketch

EX. 12

Harmonic sketch

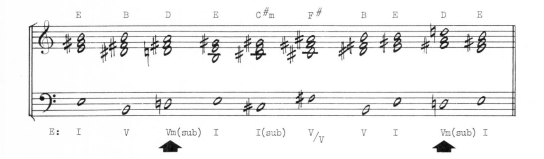

EX. 13

Harmonic sketch

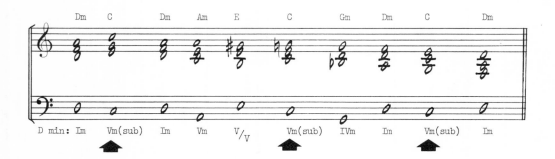

Source References

"A Hazy Shade of Winter" (P. Simon), m.1-10
"All Along the Watchtower" (B. Dylan), m.1-8
"By the Time I Get to Phoenix" (J. Webb), *coda*

"Castles Made of Sand" (J. Hendrix), m.1-8
"Cut My Hair" (D. Crosby), throughout
"High on the Mountain" (S. Katz), m.1-5
"I've Told You for the Last Time" (Cropper-Bramlett) m.41-45
"Most Anything You Want" (D. Ingle), throughout
"Never My Love" (D. Addrisi), m.1-4
"One Minute Woman" (Gibb-Gibb), m.1-9
"So Much to Say, So Much to Give" (J. Pankow), m.1-10
"Summer's Almost Gone" (The Doors), throughout
"This Guy's in Love with You" (David-Bacharach), m.1-5

Substitutions in Area Prolongation

Substitute chords are useful for prolonging and/or delaying the harmonic activity within and around a particular tonal center. Instead of simply repeating a given chord several times, substitute chords may replace the harmony—or embellish it—and the tonal influence of the chord is thereby extended. The chord of G major, for example,

EX. 14

may be adjoined by its substitutes, thus expanding the area of its influence.

EX. 15

The insertion of other harmonies to precede either the tonic chord or its substitutes will further extend the activity between the first and last chord.

EX. 16

(a)

(b) Rhythmicized

Prolongation of Tonic Area

Chords used for area prolongation must always depart from and return to the harmony that is functioning as the tone center (or "target") of the moment. Such prolongations are used when some kind of delaying action is desired prior to modulation (or other deviation) from the stated tonal center.

EX. 17

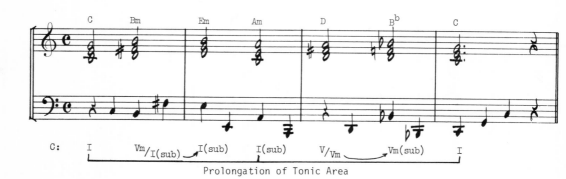

Prolongation of Tonic Area

EX. 18

Harmonic sketch

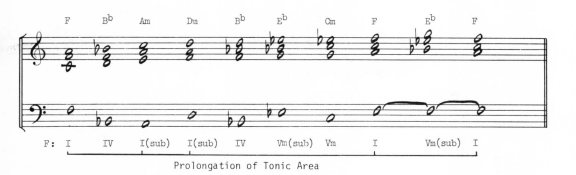

Prolongation of Tonic Area

Source References

"Does Anybody Really Know What Time It Is" (R. Lamm), m.27-39

"Movin' In" (J. Pankow), m.1-5

"Sunshine, Sunshine" (J. Taylor), m.23-32

"Sweet Baby James" (J. Taylor), m.1-13

"You're Lost Little Girl" (The Doors), m.1-12

Following are additional source references that provide varied examples of the use of substitute chords (as indicated):

"Country Girl" (N. Young), m.50-54 ($I_{m_{sub}}$, IV_{sub})

"Cut My Hair" (D. Crosby), m.7-13 (I_{sub}, $IV_{m_{sub}}$, $V_{m_{sub}}$)

"How Can I Be Sure" (Cavaliere-Brigati), *coda* ($I_{m_{sub}}$, $IV_{m_{sub}}$)

"Lady of the Island" (G. Nash), m.31-35 (I_{sub}, IV_{sub})

"Listen" (R. Lamm), m.11-20 ($I_{m_{sub}}$, $V_{m_{sub}}$)

"Little Wing" (J. Hendrix), m.1-9 (Im$_{sub}$, IVm$_{sub}$)

"Scarborough Fair/Canticle" (Simon-Garfunkel), m.1-8 (Im$_{sub}$, Vm$_{sub}$)

"Something in the Way She Moves" (J. Taylor), m.5-11 (Im$_{sub}$, Vm$_{sub}$)

"Steppin' Stone" (Boyce-Hart), m.1-12 (Im$_{sub}$, IVm$_{sub}$)

"Sunshine of Your Love" (Bruce-Brown-Clapton), m.19-25 (Im$_{sub}$, Vm$_{sub}$)

"Wintertime Love" (The Doors), m.8-16 (Im$_{sub}$, IVm$_{sub}$, Vm$_{sub}$)

"Yes the River Knows" (The Doors), 11-14 (Im$_{sub}$, IVm$_{sub}$)

Substitution in the Deceptive Cadence and "Fade coda"

The I(sub) also is used traditionally in the so-called "deceptive" cadence, where the expected tonic chord is replaced by its substitute derived from the VIm.

EX. 19

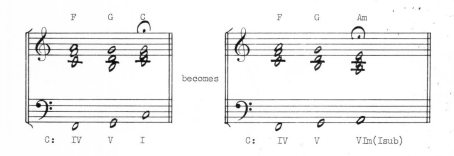

This device appears occasionally in rock harmonic progressions:

EX. 20

Harmonic sketch.

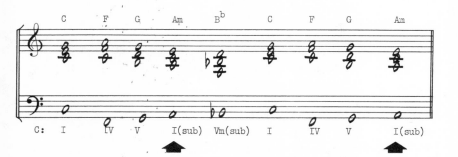

EX. 21

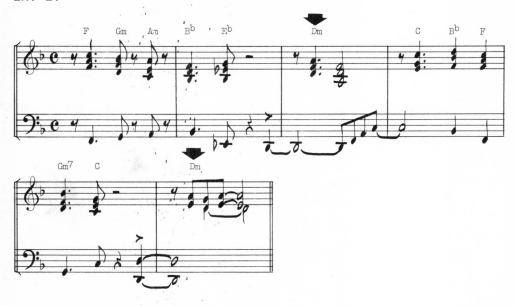

Harmonic sketch

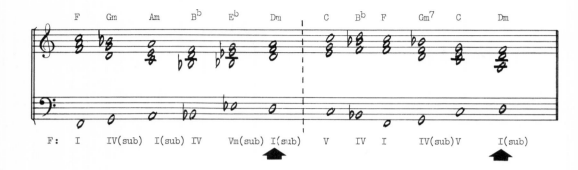

Source References

"All Along the Watchtower" (B. Dylan), throughout
"Heart of Stone" (Jagger-Richard), m.4-5; 10-11; 16-17; 22-23;
 coda
"In the Summer of His Years" (Gibb-Gibb), m.5-9
"I Want to Hold Your Hand" (Lennon-McCartney), m.1-3; 13-15;
 36-42
"I'm Happy Just to Dance with You" (Lennon-McCartney), *coda*
"If I'd Been a Different Man" (J. Webb), m.6-10, final cadence
"Liberation" (J. Pankow), m.10-14
"Most Anything You Want" (D. Ingle), m.10-12
"Something" (G. Harrison), m.6-7; 41-42

The *fade coda* is apparently an outgrowth of the tendency
in many rock progressions to emphasize ambiguity and evasive-
ness. A large number of rock compositions never reach a final
cadence, deceptive or otherwise. The player is simply directed to
"repeat and fade"—to play the final two or four measures of the
piece over and over, softer with each repetition, until the music
becomes inaudible.

Harmonic formulae for such codas vary, but in many
cases the final chord will not be tonic harmony. Typical final
chords include the following:

I(sub)	IVm(sub)
IV	V
IV(sub)	Vm(sub)

EX. 22   (Repeat and fade)

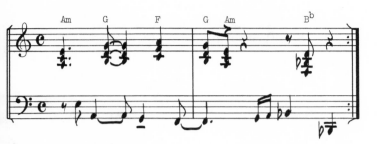

Harmonic sketch

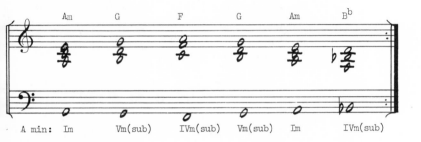

EX. 23   (Repeat and fade)

Harmonic sketch

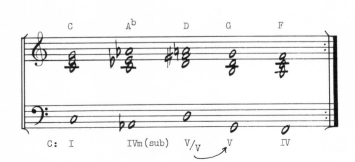

Source References

I(sub) Final: "Stand" (S. Stewart)
"Wedding Bell Blues" (L. Nyro)
"Who'll Stop the Rain" (J. Fogerty)

IV Final: "Country Girl" (N. Young)
"Cut My Hair" (D. Crosby)
"I Don't Know Why" (Bramlett-Clapton)
"In the Midnight Hour" (Pickett-Cropper)
"Poorboy Shuffle" (J. Fogerty)
"We've Only Just Begun" (Williams-Nichols)

IV(sub) Final: "Everything Is Good About You"
(Holland-Dean)
"Good Day Sunshine" (Lennon-McCartney)
"Groovin" (Cavaliere-Brigati)
"Hideaway" (J. Fogerty)
"Punky's Dilemma" (P. Simon)
"Summer's Daughter" (J. Webb)

IVm(sub) Final: "My World Is Empty Without You"
(Holland-Dozier)
"One Minute Woman" (Gibb-Gibb)

V Final: "Everyday People" (S. Stewart)
"Indian Gin and Whiskey Dry" (Gibb-Gibb)
"People Got to Be Free" (Cavaliere-Brigati)
"So Many Stars" (Lobo-DeMoraes)
"The Road" (T. Kath)
"Whiskey Man" (J. Entwhistle)

Vm(sub) Final: "Beginnings" (R. Lamm)
"Fire and Rain" (J. Taylor)
"Five to One" (The Doors)
"Kilburn Towers" (Gibb-Gibb)
"Love Is a Beautiful Thing"
(Cavaliere-Brigati)
"Love Street" (The Doors)
"Most Anything You Want" (D. Ingle)

Nine

Chromaticism and Diatonic/Mixed-Diatonic Harmony

Numerous passages in rock compositions rely upon conventional progression patterns that are adaptations of traditional harmonic practices. Such passages generally emphasize either some form of chromatic harmony or diatonic/mixed-diatonic progressions (defined in Part I, Chapter 2).

The harmonization of chromatic lines usually results in short fill-ins between, or approaches to, important chords (I, IV, or V) of the key or tonality of the moment.

EX. 1

Harmonic sketch

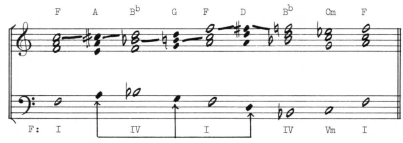

Chromatic Fill-ins Between I and IV

EX. 2

Harmonic sketch

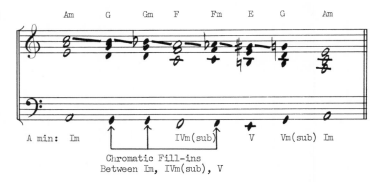

Chromatic Fill-ins
Between Im, IVm(sub), V

 Some rock pieces have borrowed chromatic clichés of the type found in conventional romantic ballads such as *My Funny Valentine, The Summer Knows,* and *What Are You Doing the Rest of Your Life.* A descending chromatic bass line is the more common form.

EX. 3

Chromatic Prolongation of the
Im-IVm Area

The same type of linear motion frequently occurs within inner parts.

EX. 4

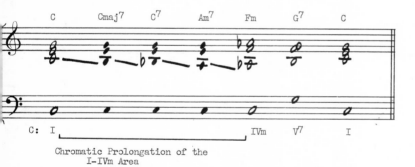

Chromatic Prolongation of the
I-IVm Area

Source References

"Deja Vu" (D. Crosby), m.27-33
"Dock of the Bay" (Cropper-Redding), m.5-11
"How Can I Be Sure" (Cavaliere-Brigati), m.20-25
"I, Me, Mine" (G. Harrison), m.25-31
"Long after Tonight Is Over" (David-Bacharach), m.9-13
"Love Street" (The Doors), m.9-16
"Move Over and Make Room for Me" (David-Bacharach), m.9-13
"Something" (G. Harrison), m.1-4; 7-10
"Things We Said Today" (Lennon-McCartney), m.33-40

Chordal modal interchange (already discussed in Part I, Chapter 5, and Part II, Chapter 6, **Summary/Addenda**) should be mentioned again since the alternation or exchange of any major harmony with the minor harmony on the same root (or substitute therefor) is essentially a chromatic operation.

EX. 5

Harmonic sketch

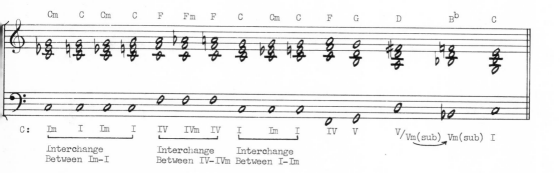

EX. 6

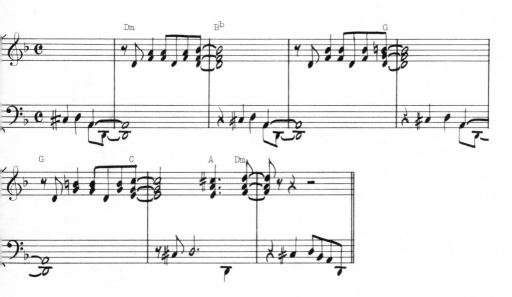

Harmonic sketch

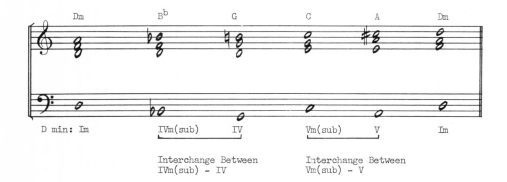

Source References

"Country Girl" (N. Young), m.1-4; 12-15; 58-61
"Deja Vu" (D. Crosby), m.19-20; 35-36
"I'm Losing You" (Grant-Whitfield-Holland), throughout
"Love Is a Beautiful Thing" (Cavaliere-Brigati), m.1-10
"Nowhere Man" (Lennon-McCartney), m.26-32
"Satisfaction" (Jagger-Richard), m.13; 15; 27; 36
"Steppin' Stone" (Boyce-Hart), m.1-7
"Taking It In" (J. Taylor), throughout
"You Keep Me Hanging On" (Holland-Dozier), m.4-5; 8-9; 21-23
    coda

Diatonic/mixed-diatonic harmonizations are found fre
quently in rock compositions of the 60s, especially the early 60s
Although such progressions contribute little that is unusual o
unique, they are nevertheless a common technique employed by
some rock composers. General categories include

IV-V-I
Secondary dominants
Stepwise diatonic area prolongations.

IV-V-I

It is assumed that no explanation is needed for this pro
gression. The following source references use the pattern fre
quently.

Source References

"Blowing in the Wind" (B. Dylan)
"Effigy" (J. Fogerty)
"Hey Jude" (Lennon-McCartney)
"I Can't See Nobody" (Gibb-Gibb)
"I'm Happy Just to Dance with You" (Lennon-McCartney)
"In the Summer of His Years" (Gibb-Gibb)
"I've Got to Get a Message to You" (Gibb-Gibb)
"I Want to Hold Your Hand" (Lennon-McCartney)
Jesus Christ Superstar "Everything's All Right" (Rice-Webber)
"Like a Rolling Stone" (B. Dylan)
"Life" (S. Stewart)
"Mrs. Robinson" (P. Simon)

Secondary Dominants

The conventional symmetrical pattern of the cycle of the fifth represents the root motion common to all secondary dominant relationships. In other words, any given chord may be preceded by a harmony whose root is a perfect fifth above. The chord of C_7, for example, may be approached by G_7.

EX. 7

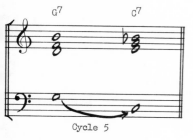

Cycle 5

The same principle applies to any other harmony. The progression appears sporadically in rock music and, in some cases, a continuous chain of secondary dominants may occur.

EX. 8

Continuous Cycle 5

Source References

"Chained and Bound" (O. Redding), m.5-9
"I Wanna Be Your Man" (Lennon-McCartney), m.18-22
"Mrs. Robinson" (P. Simon), m.21-31
"Something" (G. Harrison), m.1-6
"Spinning Wheel" (D. C. Thomas), m.1-6; 9-14

Diatonic Area Prolongations

This type of space-filling usually employs step-wise motion directly up or down the scale (tonal area) of the moment:

EX. 9

Harmonic sketch

Diatonic Prolongation of the I - IV Area

EX. 10

Harmonic sketch

Diatonic Prolongation of the I Area

EX. 11

Harmonic sketch

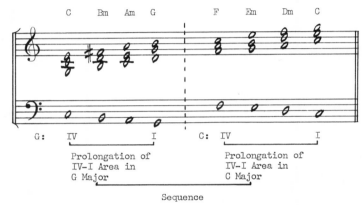

Sequence

Source References

"Awaiting on You All" (G. Harrison), m.9-14
"Fakin' It" (P. Simon), m.8-12
"Here There and Everywhere" (Lennon-McCartney), m.1-8
"If I'd Been a Different Man" (J. Webb), m.1-6
"Scarborough Fair/Canticle" (Simon-Garfunkel), m.13-18; 61-66

Ten
Characteristic Structures

One of the principal harmonic features of rock music in the 60s was the return to the triad as an integral sound term. Seventh chords, of course, were still in use, and several other structures played an important role in shaping the harmonic style of rock. Illustrations are grouped in the following categories:

> The suspended fourth *(sus 4)*
> Dominant seventh with raised ninth
> Open fourths and fifths
> Miscellaneous structures (ninths, elevenths,
>   thirteenths, and other rarely used chords)

The Suspended 4th

Use of the suspended 4th as a separate harmonic entity apparently developed from the common contrapuntal suspension of the fourth degree of a tonic chord in plagal cadences of the Renaissance and Baroque.

EX. 1

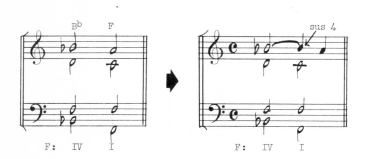

The same principle may be applied to the dominant.

EX. 2

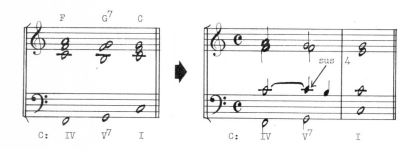

It may also be applied to any major or minor chord in tertian harmony.

EX. 3

It is necessary to generalize the concept of *sus 4* when progressions, such as the above, move away from the tone center (and/or scale) of the moment. Specifically, the tone a perfect fourth above any given chord root is considered to be the *sus 4*. Further, the *sus 4* in rock harmony is usually not resolved, but simply remains in the chord as a non-harmonic tone that *replaces* the third (major or minor).

EX. 4

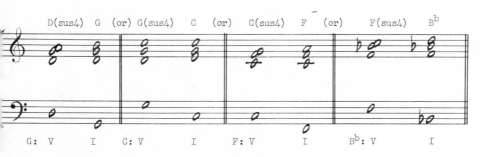

In rock compositions the *sus 4* occurs primarily on th
dominant, or in chords of a dominant-seventh-type structure. I
the chord does contain a seventh as well as a *sus 4*, the resultin
harmony has a marked subdominant quality that, typically
provides yet another way to avoid definitive dominant-toni
movement toward the tonic of the moment.

EX. 5

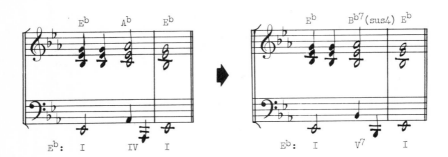

Following are additional examples of the *sus* 4:

EX. 6

Harmonic sketch

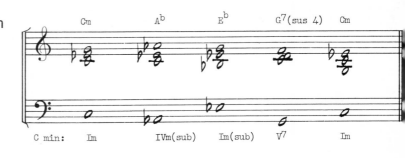

EX. 7

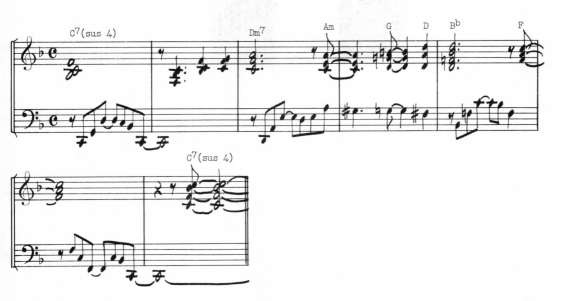

Harmonic sketch

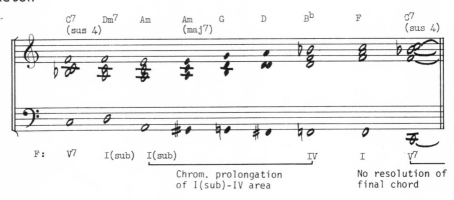

Occasional instances occur where the *sus 4* is used with chords other than the dominant.

EX. 8

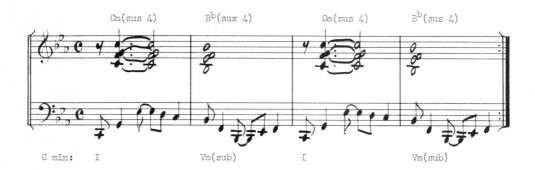

Source References

"A Beautiful Morning" (Cavaliere-Brigati), final chord (B♭ sus 4)
"Come Together" (Lennon-McCartney), m.34-35 (G7 sus 4)
"Didn't We" (J. Webb), m.1-3 (G♭ sus 4)
"I Can See for Miles" (P. Townsend), m.12-13; *coda* (non-dominant sus 4)
"I Can't See Your Face" (The Doors), throughout (non-dominant sus 4)
"Rainy Day Man" (J. Taylor), m.7-14, (D7 sus 4)
"This Guy's in Love with You" (David-Bacharach), m.16-17 (B♭ sus 4)
"You Keep Me Hanging On" (Holland-Dozier), m.13-14 (C7 sus 4)
"West Virginia Fantasies" (J. Pankow), m.1-4 (B♭ sus 4)
"Wichita Lineman" (J. Webb), m.1-3; 7-9 (C7 sus 4; D7 sus 4)

The Dominant Seventh with Raised Ninth

This structure is favored in hard rock and soul rock where a repetitive ostinato pattern is established. The chord owes its principal instability to the presence of the interval of a major seventh between the third and the raised ninth.

EX. 9

For this reason, the raised ninth chord often appears without the root, but without losing its characteristic dissonance.

EX. 10

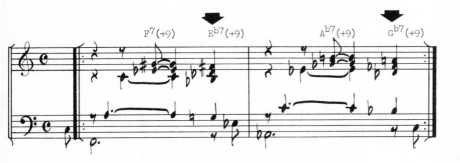

Historically, the structure may have had its origin in the Baroque cadence that was sometimes used in eighteenth century chorales. The unstable major seventh (enharmonic) interval is caused by the non-harmonic tone in the soprano.

EX. 11

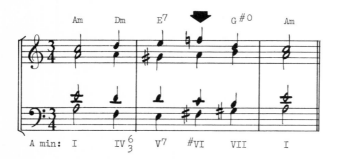

The complete dominant-seventh structure with raised ninth, however, did not become standard until the early twentieth century (see *Appendix,* Section II). It was one of the few high-tension chords of the 40s and 50s that has been retained by rock composers, especially in rhythmic ostinatos.

EX. 12

(a)

(b)

Source References

"Deja Vu" (D. Crosby), m.45-46
"Hawg for You" (O. Redding), m.16-17; 21
"I'll Go Crazy" (J. Brown), m.5; 18; 20
"Knocking Around the Zoo" (J. Taylor), m.75-80
"Liberation" (J. Pankow), throughout
"Still Raining, Still Dreaming" (J. Hendrix), throughout
"Ticket to Ride" (Lennon-McCartney), m.14-15
"Try" (Ragovoy-Taylor), m.3-4
"Turtle Blues" (Joplin), m.1-3

Open Fourths and Fifths

The coupled melodic lines of medieval parallel organum
(see the *Appendix,* Section II) were restricted to intervals of perfect fourths or fifths. The resulting structures, sometimes referred to as "incomplete triads," were not popular after about 1150,
but they began to appear again in impressionist compositions
and later in music of the rock period. There is no particular
pattern to their usage, although points of cadential activity
seem to be somewhat favored. The employment of perfect fourths
and fifths tends to emphasize the primitivistic eclecticism of
some rock pieces.

EX. 13

EX. 14

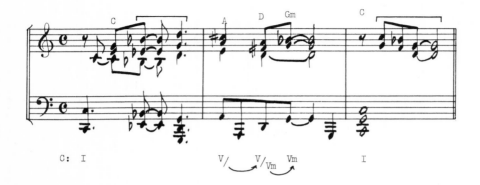

Source References

"Cut My Hair" (D. Crosby), m.13-15
"Deja Vu" (D. Crosby), m.46-48
"Five to One" (The Doors), m.55-56
"Forty-Nine Bye-Byes" (S. Stills), m.25-30
"I Can See for Miles" (P. Townsend), m.4-10; 12-13
."Lady of the Island" (G. Nash), m.18-21
"Rejoyce" (G. Slick), throughout
"The Unknown Soldier" (The Doors), m.1-4

Miscellaneous Structures

Other structures, rarely used, include ninths (dominant seventh with raised ninth excepted), elevenths, thirteenths, and an occasional diminished or augmented triad. There is even an infrequent polychord or two—usually superposed structures in thirds.

EX. 15

(a) Superposed major triads

(b) Superposed major sevenths

Since these structures (cited above) are not prevalent factors in rock harmonic technique, only materials for reference are given:

Source References

(Dim/Aug Triads)	"All My Loving" (Lennon-McCartney), m.33-35 "If I Fell" (Lennon-McCartney), m.1-3 "I'm Happy Just to Dance with You" (Lennon-McCartney), m.1-2
(Ninths, Elevenths, Thirteenths)	"Forty Thousand Headmen" (Winwood-Capaldi), m.1-12 "If I Fell" (Lennon-McCartney), m.19-21 "I Me Mine" (G. Harrison), m.17-20 "Never My Love" (D. Addrisi), final chord "Rainy Day, Dream Away" (J. Hendrix), m.9-13 "Redemption" (Thomas-Halligan), m.9; 12-13 "Things We Said Today" (Lennon-McCartney), m.36-37 "The Road" (T. Kath), m.32-37
(Polychords)	"Colour My World" (J. Pankow), final chord "Prologue" (J. Webb), *intro;* m.11-14 "Rejoyce" (G. Slick), final chord

Note should also be made of a particular and characteristic use of minor sevenths by Bert Bacharach, whose compositions have been featured by soft rock groups. This type of chord is used to support the *first principal melodic high point* in many Bacharach pieces. The device lends a clearly recognizable quality to many of the composer's works. In the following illustration the melodic high point occurs in measure 4, and a minor seventh structure provides the harmonic support:

EX. 16

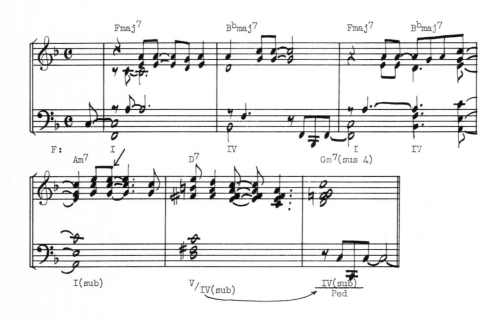

Source References

(Harmonization of first principal melodic high point with minor seventh.)

"As Long As There's an Apple Tree," m.9-10; 13-14
"Do You Know the Way to San José," m.11-13; 17-19
"Promises, Promises," m.5-6
"Raindrops Keep Fallin' on My Head," m.5-6
"The Forgotten Man," m.9-11
"The Look of Love," m.10-11
"This Guy's in Love with You," m.8-9
"What the World Needs Now," m.1-3

(All compositions by David-Bacharach.)

Eleven

Tonal Ambiguities; Density-in-Time; Sectional Form

Diminution of Key Signature Influence

The specific tonality of some rock chord progressions is frequently unpredictable and open to question. The tone center of a given progression may be subjected to literal (often banal) repetition throughout the song, or it may leap unexpectedly to keys quite removed from the opening tonality. Also, a composition (in three sharps, for example) may completely avoid the establishment of the "correct" key of A major or F# minor; or a piece in one flat may be without either an F major or D minor chord. Such aberrations, of course, are in accord with the ambiguous and evasive aspects of rock philosophy.

"Good Day Sunshine" (Lennon-McCartney) has a key signature of one sharp, but there is no G major or E minor chord throughout, and the most important tone center is A major! "How Can I Be Sure" (Cavaliere-Brigati) has a key signature of two sharps, but the modality of the melody fluctuates between A

Dorian, F major, and D minor. In "We've Only Just Begun" (Williams-Nichols), the tonality of neither B♭ major nor G minor is used to confirm the key signature of two flats; and "Make It Easy on Yourself" (David-Bacharach) employs A♭ harmony as the tonic, within the key signature of three flats. All of these situations indicate the decreasing influence of key signatures.

EX. 1

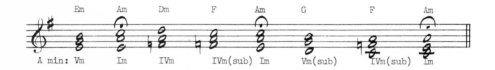

The key signature is one sharp, yet F# is not used, and the tonality of the moment is A minor.

Source Reference: "Down to Earth" (Gibb-Gibb), m.1-29

EX. 2

The key signature shows no sharps or flats, but G major tonality predominates.

Source Reference: "You Don't Have to Cry" (S. Stills), m.1-17

EX. 3

The key signature has no sharps or flats, yet the progression opens and closes with B♭ harmony.

Source Reference: "Let There Be Love" (Gibb-Gibb), m.1-10

Many compositions have traditionally appropriate key signatures, but contain progressions that are subject to more than one interpretation.

EX. 4

Roman numerology for this progression can be adapted to either D minor or F major as principal tonal areas.

EX. 5

(a)
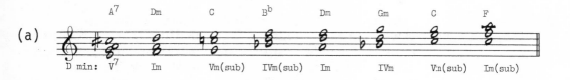

(b)

Source Reference: "Yesterday" (Lennon-McCartney), m.15-18

EX. 6

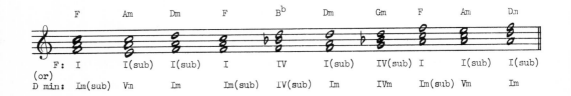

Source Reference: "A Day in the Life" (Lennon-McCartney),
m.1-6

Chordal Density-in-Time

An important subsidiary feature of rock harmonic analysis pertains to the number of different chords used in a given work—*chordal density-in-time*. The term "density" should not be confused with intervallic techniques for measuring the relative consonance or dissonance of a series of harmonies[4]. It refers, in this instance, to quantity rather than quality; to the total number of individual chords per section of a work.

A particular characteristic of many rock pieces is the use of an absolute minimum of chord structures. In such cases, a very low chordal density-in-time facilitates the repetitive, ostinato-like melodic/rhythmic figures that characterize much primitivistic hard rock, soul, and some folk rock. The tune "Cat's Squirrel" (S. Splurge, performed by Cream) contains only the single chord of C throughout; and both "Bootleg" and "Feelin' Blue" (J. Fogerty, featured by Creedence Clearwater) contain one chord in each piece: C_7 in the former and D_7 in the latter.

Other examples of compositions with varying degrees of chordal density-in-time are given in CHART I. Where possible, they should be examined in their entirety in order to appreciate the marked contrast between works with a minimal density and those that rely heavily upon a high chordal density-in-time.

Order of Sectional Recurrence

Regularity of phrase and section was a common characteristic of most popular music prior to the rock period. The length of each section was generally predictable—usually eight measures—and the order of sectional recurrence was normally AABA or ABAB.

In rock compositions, however, such conventional patterns are often altered or discarded. Songs vary in length from 11 measures ("So Much to Say, So Much to Give," J. Pankow) to 122 measures ("How Can I Be Sure," Cavaliere-Brigati); and the order of thematic and/or sectional recurrences is subject to irregularity. There is also a wide variety of measure-numbers per section, and the pacing of chord progressions in sections with an odd number of measures is variable. It is useful to compare such progressions with those occurring in sections where the number of measures is even.

CHART II provides source references for examination of typical irregular or asymmetrical formal relationships.

CHART I - Chordal Density-in-Time

Group	Composition	Total Number Harmonies in Composition	Specific Names of Harmonies				
			1 Chord	2 Chords	3 Chords	4 Chords	5 Chords
The Beatles	"All Things Must Pass" (G. Harrison)	3			Eb Ab Bbm I IV Vm		
	"Come Together" (Lennon-McCartney)	4				Cm G7 F7 Am Im V IV I (sub)	
	"Blue Jay Way" (G. Harrison)	1	C I				
The BeeGees	"Kilburn Towers" (Gibb-Gibb)	3			Em D Bm Vm Vm (sub)		
The Rolling Stones	"Satisfaction" (Jagger-Richards)	2		Eb Ab I IV			
	"Please Go Home" (Jagger-Richards)	3			G D A Vm IV I (sub)		
The Doors	"The End"	3			D C G I Vm IV (sub)		
Iron Butterfly	"Most Anything You Want" (D. Ingle)	5					C Bb Am F G I Vm I IV V (sub)
Jimi Hendrix	"Still Raining, Still Dreaming" (J. Hendrix)	1	D7(+9)				
	"Voodoo Chile" (J. Hendrix)	1	D7(+9)				
The Rascals	"People Got to Be Free" (Cavaliere-Brigati)	4				Bb F C7 F IV I V I	
James Brown	"Tell Me What You're Gonna Do" (J. Brown)	5					G7 C7 D C G V/IV IV V IV I
Otis Redding	"I'm Sick Y'All" (Redding-Cropper-Porter)	2		C Bb I Vm (sub)			
Sly and the Family Stone	"Everyday People" (S. Stewart)	2		G C I IV			
Chicago	"Movin' In" (J. Pankow)	5					C Em Am F C I I I IV I (sub)(sub)
Simon and Garfunkel	"Bookends" (P. Simon)	2		Fm7 Eb IV I (sub)			
Creedence Clearwater	"Poorboy Shuffle" (J. Fogerty)	3			C I C I IV I		
	"Bad Moon Rising" (J. Fogerty)	3			C Bb F V IV I		
	"Feelin' Blue" (J. Fogerty)	1	D7				
	"Chameleon" (J. Fogerty)	4				A G D Bm V IV I I (sub)	
Crosby, Stills, Nash, and Young	"Helpless" (N. Young)	3			D A G I V IV		
Bob Dylan	"Ballad of Hollis Brown" (B. Dylan)	1	Em I				
	"Masters of War" (B. Dylan)	2		Em D I Vm (sub)			
	"All Along the Watchtower" (B. Dylan)	3			Am F G Im IVm Vm (sub)(sub)		

CHART II - Sectional Form

Group	Composition	Sectional Form (Recurrence Pattern)	Number of Measures in Each Section	Comments
The Beatles	"I Wanna Be Your Man" (Lennon-McCartney)	A_1 A_2 B	8,8,9	Unbalanced sectional form; customary return to A omitted. Number of measures in each section irregular.
	"You're Going to Lose That Girl" (Lennon-McCartney)	A_1 A_2 B A_3	12,14,7, 15	Sectional form is conventional, but number of measures in each section is irregular.
	"I'd Have You Anytime" (Dylan-Harrison)	A_1 B A_2 Coda	10,7,5,5	Symmetrical sectional form, but number of measures in each section is irregular.
	"Something" (G. Harrison)	A_1 B A_2 Coda	9,16,9,3	Symmetrical sectional form, but number of measures in each section is irregular.
The Rolling Stones	"Lady Jane" (Jagger-Richard)	A_1 B_1 A_2 B_2	8,9,8,9	Balanced repetitive sectional form. Number of measures irregular.
	"The Lantern" (Jagger-Richard)	A_1 B_1 A_2 B_2 A_3	10,5,5,4, 4	Symmetrical sectional form, but number of measures in each section irregular in progressive diminution.
The Who	"I Can See for Miles" (P. Townsend)	A B Coda	16,25,5	Non-repetitive sectional form. Number of measures in each section irregular.
Cream	"Don't Know Why" (Bramlett-Clapton)	A_1 A_2 A_3 Coda	15,15,15, 2	Repetitive sectional form. Same number of measures in all sections (except Coda) but the number of measures per section is uneven.
The Doors	"Strange Days"	A_1 A_2	23,23	Repetitive sectional form, but number of measures per section is uneven.
	"The Crystal Ship"	A_1 A_2 Interlude A_3 A_4 Coda	13, 11,8, 13, 11,3	Repetitive sectional form. Number of measures in each section irregular. This composition is one of few with a published interlude.
Jefferson Airplane	"Rejoyce" (G. Slick)	A B C D E . . . etc.	117 measures with no repeats	No apparent sectional form. Unusually long composition. Total number of measures irregular.
Jimi Hendrix	"Little Wing" (J. Hendrix)	A_1 A_2 Coda	9,9,2	Repetitive sectional form. Number of measures per section uneven.
The Rascals	"How Can I Be Sure" (Cavaliere-Brigati)	A_1 B_1 B_2 A_2 B_3 Coda	18,32,36 12,20,4	Unusually long, with asymmetrical sectional form and different number of measures per section.
James Brown	"I'll Go Crazy" (J. Brown)	A_1 A_2 A_3 A_4	8,8,12, 12	Repetitive sectional form, but A_1 and A_2 constitute an unusual eight-measure blues form in contrast to A_3 and A_4 which employ the traditional twelve-measure form.
Sly and the Family Stone	"Stand" (S. Stewart)	A_1 A_2 A_3 A_4 Coda	11,19,11, 19,8	Repetitive sectional form with an irregular number of measures per section.
Chicago	"So Much to Say, So Much to Give" (J. Pankow)	A	11	One isolated section with an irregular number of measures per section.
The Carpenters	"We've Only Just Begun"	A_1 A_2 B A_3 Coda	8,10,9 12,4	Conventional sectional form, but with different number of measures per section.
Seals and Crofts	"Summer Breeze" (Seals-Crofts)	A_1 B C A_2	6,10,9,6	Asymmetrical sectional form. Different number of measures per section.
Simon and Garfunkel	"Bookends" (P. Simon)	A_1 A_2 Coda	9,7,10	Repetitive sectional form. Different number of measures per section.
Crosby, Stills, Nash, and Young	"Helplessly Hoping" (S. Stills)	A_1 A_2 B	11,10,6	Unbalanced sectional form. Number of measures irregular in progressive diminution.
The Association	"Never My Love" (D. Addrisi)	A B A B	8,7,8,7	Balanced sectional form, but different number of measures per section.
Burt Bacharach	"Raindrops Keep Falling" (David-Bacharach)	A_1 A_2 B A_3	9,9,10,12	Conventional section form. Different number of measures per section.
Jimmy Webb	"The Girls' Song" (J. Webb)	A_1 B_1 A_2 B_2	8,13,8,13	Balanced sectional form. Different number of measures per section.
	"If I'd Been a Different Man" (J. Webb)	A_1 A_2 B A_3	7,7,7,7	Conventional sectional form. Number of measures in each section uneven.
	"Wichita Lineman" (J. Webb)	A_1 B_1 A_2 B_2 Coda	7,10,7, 10,4	Balanced sectional form. Different number of measures per section.

Part III

Synopsis of Chord Progressions Used in the Self-Study Workbook

Part III

Synopsis of Chord Progressions Used in the Self-Study Workbook

Since the standardization and general acceptance of tertian harmony, every period of musical expression has indulged in the eclectic revival of previously used techniques. But each new period has also displayed original sound-terms and other features that characterize the particular style or idiom. Rock, like jazz, is not a musical "form." It is a way of playing. It is a verb, not a noun. The musical style of rock depends heavily upon the way the rhythm section plays, and on restrictive instrumentation, electronic volume-boosters, and highly stylized vocals.

The principal progression techniques illustrated in Part II show that the harmonic devices used in rock are not new. The various chord structures and progressions have occurred in music of other idioms and other periods. It is the author's opinion, however, that certain harmonic tendencies form a perceivable thread of events that is evident in the most striking and effective rock compositions. The majority of such events rely upon progressions involving the dominant minor, subdominant (major and minor), and substitute chords. It would also appear that the technique of chord-degree harmonization is an important source of original harmonic relationships and creative projects.

The purpose of Part III is to summarize the chord progressions and extended concepts that will be applied in the self-study workbook, *Programmed Instructional Drills and Applications for Harmonic Technique in the Rock Idiom*. The various tasks in the workbook are intended to reinforce and expand the understanding of significant chord progressions through specific application.

The workbook is divided into 15 Project-Units that can be adapted to one semester's work (one Project-Unit per week) or two semesters' work (two weeks per Project-Unit).

Twelve
Basic Cadence Patterns

The self-study workbook that accompanies this text provides sequential programmed tasks designed to develop and expand certain harmonic principles through written, self-corrected application.

The choice of particular cadence patterns for application in the workbook is based upon the following premises:

1. The principal control factors in rock chord progressions are the tonic, subdominant, and dominant harmonies. The tonic and subdominant harmonies may be major or minor; dominant harmony primarily should be minor.

2. Dominant-type *major* harmony should be restricted essentially to secondary dominant relationships or V-IV-I progressions.

3. Activation/extension of the tonic, subdominant, and dominant areas is accomplished by means of substitute chords (see next chapter).

The specific tonic, subdominant, and dominant patterns that will be used in the workbook are as follows (all examples in tonal area of *C*):

EX. 1   Vm-I or Im

(Workbook projects 1, 2, 3.)

EX. 2   V/Vm-Vm-I or Im

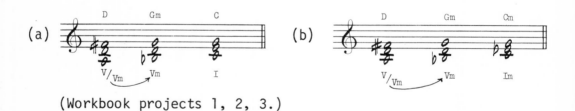

(Workbook projects 1, 2, 3.)

EX. 3   IV-I or Im

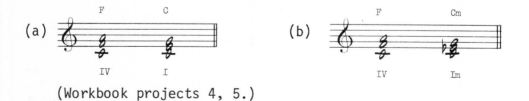

(Workbook projects 4, 5.)

EX. 4   IVm-I or Im

(a)

(b)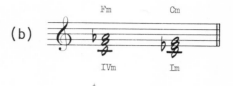

(Workbook projects 4, 5.)

EX. 5   V-IV-I or Im

(a)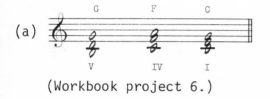

(b)

(Workbook project 6.)

EX. 6   V-IV-I or Im

(a)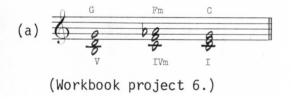

(b)

(Workbook project 6.)

EX. 7   Vm-IV-I or Im

(a)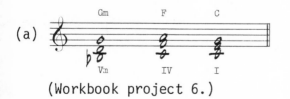

(b)

(Workbook project 6.)

EX. 8   Vm-IVm-I or Im

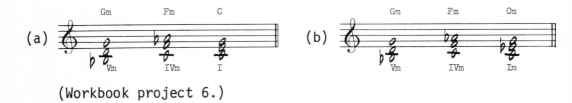

(Workbook project 6.)

EX. 9   IV-Vm-I or Im

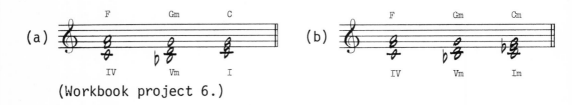

(Workbook project 6.)

Ex. 10   IVm-Vm-I or Im

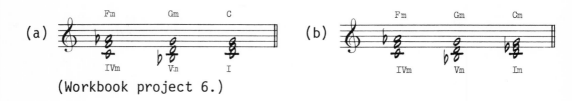

(Workbook project 6.)

Each of the above cadence formulae may be transposed to other key centers for use in a variety of tonal areas.

Thirteen

Derivation of Substitution Patterns from Basic Cadences

A firm knowledge of the basic tonic, subdominant, and dominant cadence patterns in Chapter 12 is essential to the understanding of chord substitutions, which frequently replace any or all of the chords in fundamental progressions. Not all of the available substitution patterns* will be utilized in the workbook due to the large number of possible combinations. It is important, however, to understand the general procedure for pattern evolution so that readers may experiment with a variety of possibilities too copious for inclusion in the workbook.

Definition of Elements

The principal harmonic structures of the rock period are major and minor triads. In general, all of the major and minor

---

* Workbook projects 7 through 10.

triads diatonic to major and minor keys may be regarded as tonic-, subdominant-, or dominant-type in function. This is accomplished by means of substitute chords.

In any tonal center: instead of IIm,   think IVsub
instead of VIm,   think Isub₁
instead of IIIm,   think Isub₂

instead of ♭III,   think Im(sub)
instead of ♭VIm,   think IVm(sub)₁
instead of ♭II,   think IVm(sub)₂
instead of ♭VII,   think Vm(sub)

These substitute chords—all considered to be essentially tonic-, subdominant-, or dominant-type in nature—are the core of harmonic rationalizations in the rock idiom. The following matrix should be helpful in visualizing their functions, as well as the functions of other major and minor triads that supplement and/or complement the fundamental harmonies:

EX. 1   Matrix of basic tonic, subdominant, and dominant chords, including substitutes and secondary dominants (Tonal Area of C)

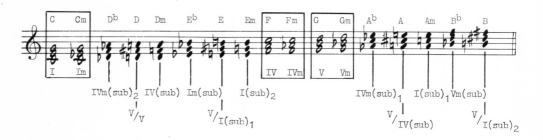

Obviously, such a variety of available major and minor harmonies within any given tonal area allows for a very large number of progression possibilities. Since—theoretically—any chord *may* progress to any other chord, players have fallen upon many combinations by chance. In order to establish specific *function,* however, all patterns should be additions/extensions, transpositions, or permutations of the basic formulae.

In summary, therefore, the basic elements of triadic rock harmony are given below. Suffix numbers simplify the identification of basic chords with more than one substitute.

I, Im, IV, IVm; Vm; V/V, V/Vm
$Isub_1$, $Isub_2$, Im(sub); $V/Isub_1$, $V/Isub_2$
IVsub, $IVm(sub)_1$, $IVm(sub)_2$; V/IVsub
Vm(sub)

A comprehensive repertory of rock progressions is developed by selectively combining the basic elements in groups of two, three, or four units. (A few combinations, including IV-V-I Vm(sub)-Im(sub), and V-IV sub are excluded.)

Combinations of Elements

Groups of two elements

V-I
-Im

IV-I
-Im

IVm-I
-Im

V-IV
-IVm

IV-Vm

IVm-Vm

Vm-IV
-IVm

$Vm-Isub_1$
$-Isub_2$
-Im(sub)

$IV-Isub_1$
$-Isub_2$
-Im(sub)

$IVm-Isub_1$
$-Isub_2$
-Im(sub)

Vm(sub)-I
-Im

IVsub-I
-Im

$IVm(sub)_1-I$
-Im

$IVm(sub)_2-I$
-Im

$Vm(sub)-Isub_1$
$-Isub_2$

$IVsub-Isub_1$
$-Isub_2$
-Im(sub)

$IVm(sub)_1-Isub_1$
$-Isub_2$
-Im(sub)

$IVm(sub)_2-Isub_1$
$-Isub_2$
-Im(sub)

$IVm(sub)_1-Vm$

$IVm(sub)_2-Vm$

IV-Vm(sub)

IVm-Vm(sub)

IVsub-Vm(sub)

$IVm(sub)_1-Vm(sub)$

$IVm(sub)_2-Vm(sub)$

Vm(sub)-IV
-IVm
-IVsub
$-IVm(sub)_1$
$-IVm(sub)_2$

Groups of three elements

V-IV-I
-Im

V-IVm-I
-Im

IV-Vm-I
-Im

IVm-Vm-I
-Im

Vm-IV-I
-Im

Vm-IVm-I
-Im

V-IVm(sub)$_1$-I
-Im

V-IVm(sub)$_2$-I
-Im

IV-Vm(sub)-I
-Im

IVm-Vm(sub)-I
-Im

IVsub-Vm(sub)-I
-Im

IVm(sub)$_1$-Vm-I
-Im

IVm(sub)$_1$-Vm(sub)-I
-Im

IVm(sub)$_2$-Vm-I
-Im

IVm(sub)$_2$-Vm(sub)-I
-Im

V/Vm-Vm(sub)-I
-Im

Vm(sub)-IV-I
-Im

Vm(sub)-IVm-I
-Im

Vm(sub)-IVsub-I
-Im

Vm(sub)-IVm(sub)$_1$-I
-Im

Vm(sub)-IVm(sub)$_2$-I
-Im

V-IV-Isub$_1$
-Isub$_2$
-Im(sub)

V-IVm-Isub$_1$
-Isub$_2$
-Im(sub)

IV-Vm-Isub$_1$
-Isub$_2$
-Im(sub)

IVm-Vm-Isub$_1$
-Isub$_2$
-Im(sub)

Vm-IV-Isub$_1$
-Isub$_2$
-Im(sub)

Vm-IVm-Isub$_1$
-Isub$_2$
-Im(sub)

V-IVm(sub)$_1$-Isub$_1$
-Isub$_2$
-Im(sub)

V-IVm(sub)$_2$-Isub$_1$
-Isub$_2$
-Im(sub)

IV-Vm(sub)-Isub$_1$
-Isub$_2$

IVm-Vm(sub)-Isub$_1$
-Isub$_2$

IVsub-Vm(sub)-Isub$_1$
-Isub$_2$

Groups of three elements (continued)

IVm(sub)$_1$-Vm(sub)-Isub$_1$
        -Isub$_2$

IVm(sub)$_2$-Vm(sub)-Isub$_1$
        -Isub$_2$

V/Vm-Vm(sub)-Isub$_1$
        -Isub$_2$

Vm(sub)-IV-Isub$_1$
        -Isub$_2$
        -Im(sub)

Vm(sub)-IVm-Isub$_1$
        -Isub$_2$
        -Im(sub)

Vm(sub)-IVsub-Isub$_1$
        -Isub$_2$
        -Im(sub)

Vm(sub)-IVm(sub)$_1$-Isub$_1$
        -Isub$_2$
        -Im(sub)

Vm(sub)-IVm(sub)$_2$-Isub$_1$
        -Isub$_2$
        -Im(sub)

Groups of four elements

V/V-V-IV-I
        -Im

V/V-V-IVm-I
        -Im

V/Vm-Vm-IV-I
        -Im

V/Vm-Vm-IVm-I
        -Im

V/Vm-Vm(sub)-IV-I
        -Im

V/Vm-Vm(sub)-IVm-I
        -Im

V/Vm-Vm(sub)-IVsub-I
        -Im

V/Vm-Vm(sub)-IVm(sub)$_1$-I
        -Im

V/Vm-Vm(sub)-IVm(sub)$_2$-I
        -Im

V/IVsub-IVsub-Vm(sub)-I
        -Im

V/IVsub-IV-Vm(sub)-I
        -Im

V/V-V-IV-Isub$_1$
        -Isub$_2$
        -Im(sub)

V/V-V-IVm-Isub$_1$
        -Isub$_2$
        -Im(sub)

V/Vm-Vm(sub)-IV-Isub$_1$
        -Isub$_2$
        -Im(sub)

V/Vm-Vm(sub)-IVm-Isub$_1$
        -Isub$_2$
        -Im(sub)

V/Vm-Vm(sub)-IVsub-Isub$_1$
        -Isub$_2$
        -Im(sub)

Groups of four elements (continued)

V/Vm-Vm(sub)-IVm(sub)$_2$-Isub$_1$
                              -Isub$_2$
                              -Im(sub)

V/IVsub-IVsub-Vm(sub)-Isub$_1$
                              -Isub$_2$

V/IVsub-IV-Vm(sub)-Isub$_1$
                           -Isub$_2$

IV-V/Vm-Vm-I
              -Im

IVm-V/Vm-Vm-I
               -Im

IV-V/Vm-Vm(sub)-I
                   -Im

IVm-V/Vm-Vm(sub)-I
                    -Im

IVsub-V/Vm-Vm(sub)-I
                      -Im

IVm(sub)$_1$-V/Vm-Vm(sub)-I
                            -Im
IVm(sub)$_2$-V/Vm-Vm(sub)-I
                            -Im
IV-V/Vm-Vm(sub)-Isub$_1$
                         -Isub$_2$

IVm-V/Vm-Vm(sub)-Isub$_1$
                          -Isub$_2$

IVsub-V/Vm-Vm(sub)-Isub$_1$
                            -Isub$_2$

IVm(sub)$_1$-V/Vm-Vm(sub)-Isub$_1$
                                  -Isub$_2$

IVm(sub)$_2$-V/Vm-Vm(sub)-Isub$_1$
                                  -Isub$_2$

Also, additional four-element groups may be formed by adding V/Isub$_1$ or V/Isub$_2$ to any three-element group that terminates with Isub$_1$ or Isub$_2$.

For example;

IV-Vm-Isub₁ → IV-Vm-V/Isub₁-Isub₁
(or)
Vm(sub)-IVm-Isub₂ → Vm(sub)-IVm-V/Isub₂-Isub₂
(or)
IVm(sub)₂-Vm(sub)-Isub₁ → IVm(sub)₂-Vm (sub)
                                    -V/Isub₁-Isub₁

Further, it should be remembered that, since a chord and its substitution are interchangeable, the secondary dominant of a substitute chord may resolve to the *original* chord.

For example;

V/IVsub may actually resolve as V/IVsub-IV; or
V/Isub₁ may actually resolve as V/Isub₁-I; or
V/Isub₂ may actually resolve as V/Isub₂-I

And the secondary dominant of any given chord may resolve to its *substitute*.

V/Vm may actually resolve as V/Vm-Vm(sub); or
V/IVm may actually resolve as V/IVm-IVm(sub)₁; or
V/IVm may actually resolve as V/IVm-IVm(sub)₂

Ideally, all of the above patterns should be realized in musical notation and played on a keyboard instrument or guitar. Following are a few selective realizations (tonal area of *C*). Note that *any final chord* of *any original group* may also be used to start the progression:

From groups with three elements

EX. 2

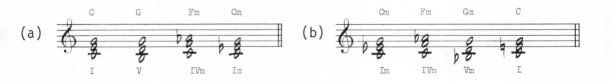

(a) C — G — Fm — Cm / I — V — IVm — Im

(b) Cm — Fm — Gm — C / Im — IVm — Vm — I

EX. 3

(a)   (b)

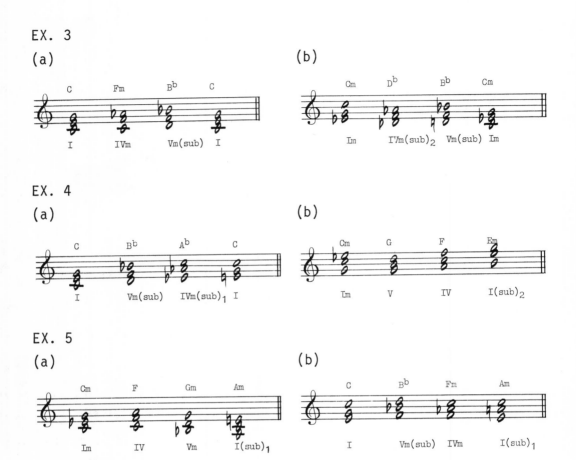

EX. 4

(a)   (b)

EX. 5

(a)   (b)

From groups with four elements

EX. 6

(a)   (b)

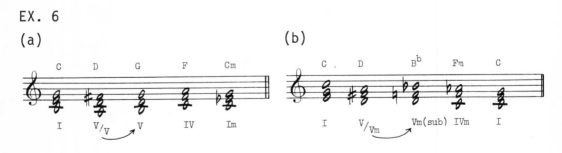

EX. 7

(a)   (b)

EX. 8

(a)   (b)

EX. 9

(a)   (b)

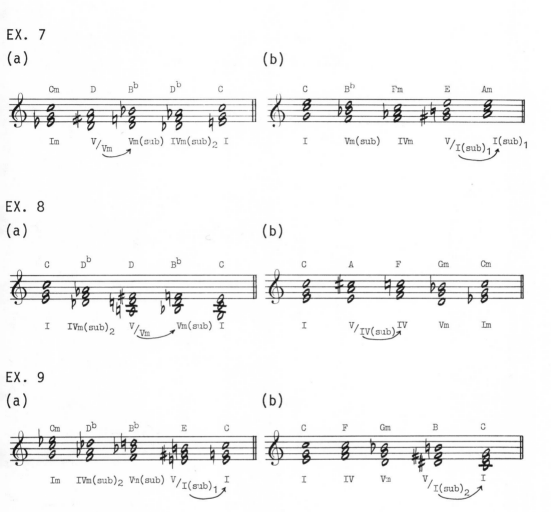

Variations

All of the progressions given above are subject to variations. Generally, the common categories of variations are:

1. Direct transposition to other key centers, either major or minor.

2. Grouping by *repetition* of units within the *same* progression, or by *combining* units from *different* progressions to form longer patterns.

3. Permutation of single units and pairs of units.

4. Modulation by means of common chords.

Transposition

EX. 10

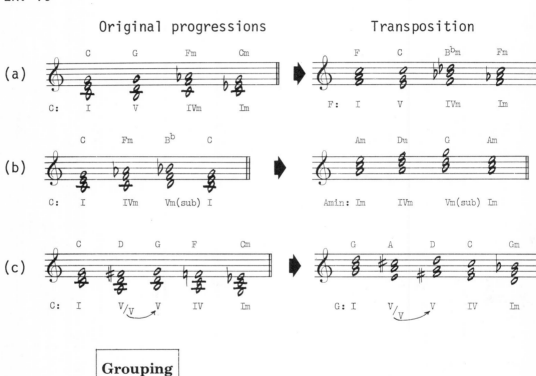

Original progressions   Transposition

Grouping

EX. 11

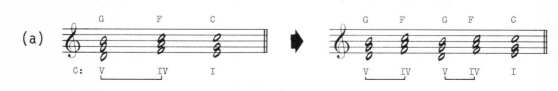

Original progressions   Repetition of two-chord unit

(b)

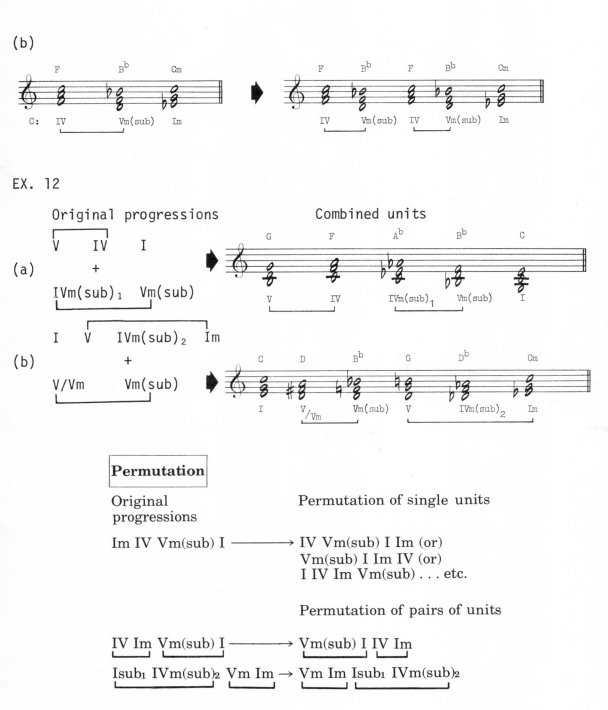

EX. 12

Original progressions   Combined units

(a)

```
   ┌─────┐
   V    IV    I
         +
IVm(sub)₁  Vm(sub)
└──────────────┘
```

(b)

```
           ┌────────────┐
I    V    IVm(sub)₂   Im
         +
V/Vm          Vm(sub)
└──────────────┘
```

Permutation

Original progressions	Permutation of single units
Im IV Vm(sub) I ──────→	IV Vm(sub) I Im (or)
	Vm(sub) I Im IV (or)
	I IV Im Vm(sub) . . . etc.

Permutation of pairs of units

IV Im Vm(sub) I ──────→ Vm(sub) I IV Im

Isub₁ IVm(sub)₂ Vm Im → Vm Im Isub₁ IVm(sub)₂

Modulation by Common Chords

EX. 13

(a) From C to A♭

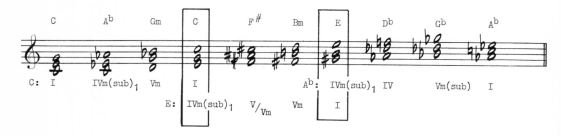

(b) From F to A

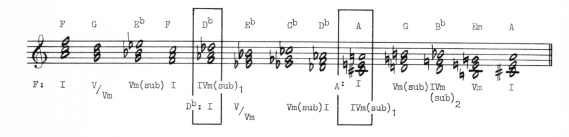

Fourteen

Extended Concepts; Expansion of Chord-Degree Harmonization Principles

The third source of chord progressions used in the workbook is based upon the technique (introduced in Part I, Chapter 3) known as "chord-degree harmonization." The basic cadence patterns and substitute chord progressions described in Chapters 12 and 13 of this part are essentially realizations of real or implied *root* movements. Chord-degree harmonization is applied to principal *melodic* tones, and provides the player with a ready source of "instant" harmony. Regardless of the melodic tone at hand, one has to consider that tone to be the root or third or fifth of a major or minor chord and add harmony accordingly. The technique is especially useful for the rock guitarist or keyboard player who seeks a variety of harmonizations that form non-conventional chord progressions.

It is necessary, however, to establish a means of exploring chord-degree harmonization patterns in an orderly fashion. This is accomplished in the workbook by developing the five concepts introduced in Part I, Chapter 3. Control of patterns to conform to key-oriented progressions is also covered. The concepts are summarized here as they will be used in the workbook:*

> I: Any single melodic tone may be assigned the chord-degree of 1 or 3 or 5 and harmonized with a major or minor triad.

> II: The assignment of chord-degrees may be applied to sustained tones.

> III: The order of assignment of the chord-degrees may be constant or variable.

> IV: Chord-degrees may be assigned to directional tones.

> V: Chord-degrees may be assigned to repeated, exchanged or combined directional tones.

I. Harmonization of Single Tones

Melodic source: Major scale on *C*.

EX. 1

Selected tone-groups: Each single tone of the scale repeated three times.

EX. 2

---

*Workbook reference: projects 11 through 15.

Chord-degree pattern: 1, 3, 5 (repeated).

*Harmonization:** Constant major structures.

EX. 3

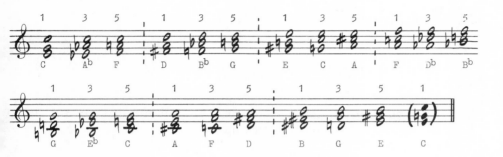

The procedure may be repeated:

(a) with constant minor structures, and

(b) in selected keys—up to three flats or three sharps is recommended (including relative minor).

II. Harmonization of Sustained Tones

Melodic source: Major scale on *F*.

EX. 4

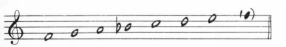

---

*All patterns should be played on guitar or keyboard (chord root doubled in left hand). Allow approximately two moderate tempo beats per chord.

Selected tone-groups: Each single tone of the scale sustained in groups of three.

EX. 5

Chord-degree pattern: 1, 3, 5 (repeated).

Harmonization: Alternation of constant minor-constant major with each tone-group.

EX. 6

The procedure may be repeated:

(a) with alternating constant major-constant minor chords with each tone-group, and

(b) in selected keys.

III. Harmonization of Single or Sustained Tones in Variab Order

Melodic source: Major scale on *G*.

EX. 7

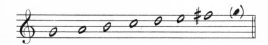

Selected tone-groups: Single and sustained tones in groups of three.

EX. 8

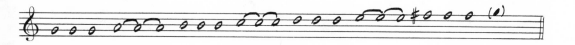

Chord-degree pattern: 1, 3, 5, in variable order.

Harmonization: Constant major structures.

EX. 9

The procedure may be repeated:

(a) with constant minor structures, and
(b) in selected keys.

IV. Harmonization of Directional Tones

Melodic source: Directional units* into the root, third, and fifth of the tonic triad (tonal center, *C*).

EX. 10   Tonic Triad

(a) Directional tones into the root

(b) Directional tones into the third

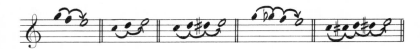

(c) Directional tones into the fifth

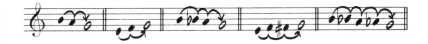

Selected tone-groups: Patterns shown in (b) above.

Chord-degree pattern: Variable.

Harmonization: Alternation of constant major-constant minor in each group (in brackets) of directional units (only). The final chord is major since it is the given "target" harmony.

---

*Embellishment patterns on the tonic triad are taken from Part I, Chapter 3. Patterns for directional tone ornamentation of the subdominant and dominant are given in the same chapter.

EX. 11

The procedure may be repeated:

(a) with directional units into root, third, or fifth of the subdominant triad;

(b) with directional units into root, third, or fifth of the dominant triad; and

(c) on other selected tonal centers.

Similar directional unit patterns are available on minor chords.

EX. 12   Tonal center of <u>C</u> minor, principal chords

EX. 13   Addition of directional units to the tonic minor chord

(a) Into the root

(b) Into the third (lowered)

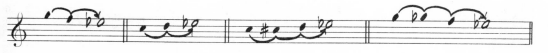

(c) Into the fifth

EX. 14   Addition of directional units to the subdominant minor chord

(a) Into the root

(b) Into the third (lowered)

(c) Into the fifth

EX. 15   Addition of directional units to the dominant minor chord

(a) Into the root

(b) Into the third (lowered)

(c) Into the fifth

These patterns may be worked out on other tonal centers and harmonized in a manner similar to Ex. 11.

V. Harmonization of Repeated, Exchanged, or Combined Directional Tones

Melodic source: Repeated, exchanged, or combined directional units into the tonic, subdominant, and dominant triads (tonal center, *C*).

Selected tone-groups: Patterns shown below.

Chord-degree patterns: Variable.

Harmonization: Major or minor, variable choice.

EX. 16

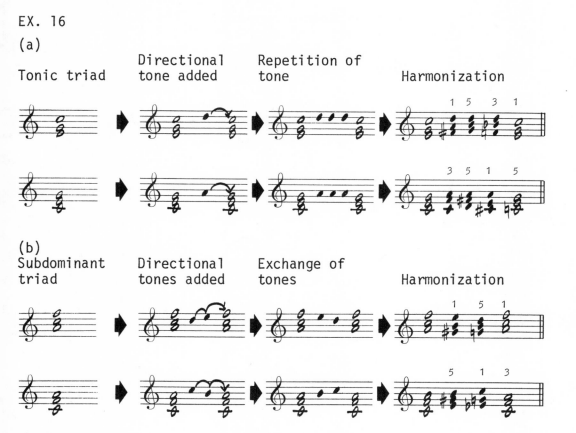

(c)

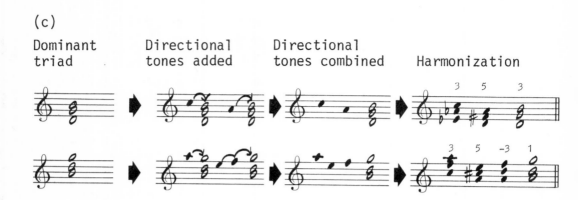

Dominant triad   Directional tones added   Directional tones combined   Harmonization

The procedure may be repeated:

- (a) with directional units into tones of the tonic minor triad;

- (b) with directional units into tones of the subdominant minor triad;

- (c) with directional units into tones of the dominant minor triad; and

- (d) on other selected tonal centers.

Appendix

Appendix
Historical Perspective

Trends in twentieth century composition, including the popular pieces of the rock period, are largely a result of accumulated knowledge and technique from earlier periods. An awareness of these trends provides a perspective for the appreciation of contemporary styles and devices.

Generally, it is not possible to examine the compositional tendencies of past times without a consideration of European influences. The mainstreams of musical effort in Western civilization took shape on the Continent, and the lasting effect of principal Continental developments is still evident in the United States.

The rock period of the 1960s was not the first time in the twentieth century that an explosive reaction took place against prevalent musical mores. The period from 1905 to 1925 contained many striking similarities. In Paris and Vienna, for example, the forces of Impressionism and Expressionism became well enough established to affect, or control, the predominating musical thrusts in the Western world and to form the foundation of the complex aggregate of phenomena currently termed "American music."

European Impressionism contributed its harmonic structures to jazz and the American popular love song, and became the wellspring of American film music, theater music, and the entire "big band" era. The inward-turning, highly intellectualized, psychical convolutions of the Schönberg *(et al.)* expressionist movement laid the aesthetic bases for various cerebral sound-experiments and removed the last vestiges of tonal restraint from the scores of composers no longer concerned with popular communication. The tonal ambiguities, rhythmic freedom, and chaos-building intensity of the rock medium are directly related to certain aspects of the expressionist movement.

Section I

Rock as Expressionism

The essence of Expressionism is distortion. Caricature contains the exaggerated emphasis that parodies reality, yet suggests a genuine quality of artistic concern. The vehicle of Expressionism's successful communication is shock; the observer is literally forced to give heed because of the manner in which the subject material is treated. In twentieth century expressionistic operas such as Berg's *Lulu* and *Wozzeck* (in which themes of human misery and degradation predominate), the composer relies on the self-defeating oppressiveness of morbidity to stimulate a reluctant empathy in the listener. Expressionism, in all cases, is uncompromising, demanding, and possessive. It asks no quarter and expects the undivided attention of its audience.

The hard rock ensemble achieves distortion and shock through acoustical intensity-variations and electronically synthesized changes of instrumental timbre. Powerful over-amplification obviates any possibility of interference, and the players are enclosed within a great wall of sound, often enhanced by a maze of psychedelic lighting. The fact that the establishment is turned aside by the formidable barrier is ideal, since the rock-cultist wants no alien encroachment upon his exclusive world. Rejection of the norm is clearly displayed through costuming, pageantry, hair styles and the adoption of irrelevant or historical pseudonyms (Jefferson Airplane, Grateful Dead, The Who, Chicago Transit Authority, etc.), and the turning away from outer reality by the use of mind-bending drugs.

Another device that certifies the "exclusiveness" of rock is the deliberate ambiguity in the music itself. The conventional ABAB or AABA even-measured form of the popular romantic song has given way to a loose form that may or may not have repeats, and that often contains a variable number of measures in adjacent sections. "Rejoyce" (1967), by the Jefferson Airplane, has 117 measures without a repeat; "I'd Have You Anytime" (1970), by George Harrison, contains ten-, seven-, and five-measure phrases with a non-vocal instrumental coda of five measures. Also standard is a coda that has no definite ending but is simply "faded" by endless repetitions that gradually grow softer and die out completely. Nonsense syllables and meaningless word sequences have been deliberately employed as a rejection of conventional communication procedures. The late Jim Morrison of The Doors states, "I am interested in anything about disorder, chaos, especially activity which seems to have no meaning";[1] and author Paul Nelson, referring to Morrison's vocals, speaks of "the shreiks (sic) and screams" that "come from a subconscious layer under the conscious artistry . . . ."[2]

Chord progressions, also, are handled in an unorthodox manner. The usual dominant-tonic cadences are deliberately avoided; substitute chords replace the conventional harmonies of traditional popular progressions; and chord-degree harmonizations create patterns of equivocal, digressive, and tangential harmonic motion.

In all instances, serious rock in the 1960s centered on tortuous, internal "revelations" that had special significance for the players and their followers. The medium became a vehicle for the dissemination of deliberately obscure precepts that were intended to close out establishment listeners. Distortion, shock effects, and a controlled neuroticism heightened the sense of exclusion, and certain devices of ambiguity in the melodic, harmonic, and rhythmic structure of the music provided the means for structuring a completely subjective tonal environment.

Rock musicians' lives became performances. Many of them adopted bizarre costumes and concentrated on acting out roles that parodied the pageantry and stylized dress of the past. Beards, long hair, exotic clothes, and posed daguerreotype-like portraits became standard props. Dance styles emphasized sex, separateness, and the harsh, physical aspects of the music. Rock, as a reflection of a total life-style, was a symbolic language—an "identity vehicle."[3] It became the expression of a complete, and essentially separate, subculture with its own set of values.

Rock as Primitivism

Historically, the expressionistic qualities of rock may be regarded as a latter-day reflection of tendencies that have prevailed throughout the history of art, and that were a leading force in atonal music of the early twentieth century. However, another important aesthetic aspect of the idiom should not be overlooked: it centered on a revival of Primitivism.

Collections of rock songs that include instrumental parts for guitarists are probably the first examples of twentieth-century anthologies containing the assurance on the cover that "You don't have to read music to play the solos in this book." Such a statement is possible since the guitar accompaniment may be written in tablature, indicating the string to be played, the specific number of the fret, and the rhythm.

X. 1

uitar

This kind of "finger notation" is quite similar to some Italian and Spanish lute tablatures of the sixteenth century, and it clearly points up the lack of technical background of many self-taught players in rock groups.

Relatively untrained guitarists are also faced with th
problem of reading music in unfamiliar keys. But by using th
"capo fret," which automatically raises the tuning of the entir
instrument, performers can "read" in a simple key while actu
ally sounding chords of the key a minor third (or some othe
interval) above the original tonality.

Predictably, musicians who need tablature notation an
use the capo fret for changing keys may be inclined towar
modes of expression less sophisticated than those that normall
prevail in Western music. The art of primitive cultures usuall
displays characteristics that appear as common factors in bot
painting and music. These include simplicity of line, continuou
repetition of ideas, superimposition (overlays) of rhythmic de
sign, a deep interest in eroticism, and the use of folk influence
and traditions as a source of inspiration. Also, modern tender
cies toward primitivistic expression are frequently influenced b
the exotic elements of Asian and Oriental art that first filtere
into European society through international expositions such a
the one in Paris in 1899. There, the effect of two-dimensiona
Japanese painting and Javanese gamelan music had a profoun
effect upon impressionist artists and upon the leading im
pressionist composer of France, Claude Debussy.

By 1910, the European movement towards Primitivisr
had gained a new champion—Igor Stravinsky. His *Firebir*
Suite, based on a fantasized folk-tale of pagan Russia, leane
heavily upon exoticism, simplicity of melodic line, polyrhythm
and ostinato. But it was Stravinsky's *Le Sacre du Printemp*
(The Rite of Spring) that discarded the last vestiges of im
pressionistic influence and fell upon Paris, as Jean Cocteau said
"comme une bombe." *The Rite of Spring* was a recountal o
primitive customs in Russia about 400 B.C. It startled the over
civilized artists of Paris with its barbarian force and violence. I
shattered an era of sophistication and established Primitivisr
as a form of idiomatic expression. Immediacy, simplicity of line
repetitive ideas through melodic and percussive rhythmic *osti*
nato, superposition of rhythmic and harmonic strata, and th
reliance upon folk mythology were prominently displayed.

Rhythmic ostinato is an ever-present factor in rock. Th
percussive use of this device creates the pulsative power tha
underlies the distinctive rock beat, and the fractione
periodicities that make up the various rhythmic layers are th
result of a gradual increase, through the years, in the intensit
of the attack patterns being used. During the periods of earl
jazz and the swing era, a basic quarter-note beat was overlaid b
melodic patterns in which the eighth-note predominated. Wit

the appearance of rhythm and blues in the 1950s, the eighth-note subdivisions of the beat gave way to background rhythm subdivisions in triplets, which became a principal part of the patterns played by the rhythm section. In the 1960s, rock drummers produced further intensity by introducing, and sustaining, a dominating attack pattern of sixteenth-note subdivisions of the beat.

The expressionistic and primitivistic aspects of rock are, of course, overlapping phenomena, but their characteristics can be differentiated. Expressionistically, the rock performer became an image of escape, an object for the emotional transfer of the anxieties and frustrations of his listeners. Distortion, shock, mind-bending drugs, and psychedelia became expressive media in themselves; inner exclusiveness was outwardly enhanced by the deliberate use of ambiguity and the exploitation of non-meaning.

Primitivism, by contrast, concerns the use of techniques from past times, such as repetitive ideas, ostinato, and chords of incomplete structure or low tension.[4] The socio-philosophical characteristics of the rock movement cannot directly control the melodic, rhythmic and harmonic techniques that are essential factors in the music itself. They do, however, control the attitudes of the performers and their audience. They also affect the musical decisions of the composers, and give perspective to the understanding of technical devices chosen as means of expression.

Section II

Trends and Motivational Forces in Earlier Periods; The Historical Development of Chord Structures

An understanding of the historical trends that have contributed directly or indirectly to the music of our time, and therefore to the rock idiom, is important to the acquisition of general musical perspective.

Rock, like any other musical idiom, is set against the backdrop of previous development. The rock phenomenon was heir to several of the influences and sound-terms from previous eras. Its specific place in history becomes more significant as analysis reveals the relationship between typical rock devices and those that were popular in earlier days.

Stylistic trends from the Middle Ages to the twentieth century can be correlated with certain changes in the growth of chord structures; and a survey of past harmonic practices emphasizes the developmental forces that had a major effect on the evolution of vertical sonorities.

For purposes of this study, the principal musical periods of Western civilization music have been separated into six general areas:

The Period of Medieval Conformity
(c. 600-1300)
The Period of Renaissance Individualism
(c. 1450-1600)
The Period of Baroque Expansion
(c. 1600-1750)
The Period of Classical Equilibrium
(c. 1750-1825)
The Period of Romantic Emotionalism
(c. 1825-1910)
The Period of Twentieth-Century Reaction
(c. 1890-present)

A brief examination of each of these periods will provide highly condensed and readily available information that outlines the mainstream of events in our musical past.

The Period of Medieval Conformity
(Principal Musical Development: Organum)

The restrictive life-style of the Middle Ages was directly reflected in the artistic activity of the period. The subject matter of the visual arts of the time was almost completely subjugated to the needs and dictates of the Roman church. Paintings were primarily of religious scenes, personages, and events. The major architectural achievements were the churches, culminating in the twelfth and thirteenth centuries with the great gothic cathedrals of France; the principal role of sculpture was the internal and external adornment of these edifices.

Secular music in the Middle Ages—troubadour-trouvère songs, instrumental dances, and the like—was, of course, widespread. But the major works were sacred and were written for the ecclesiastical hierarchy; the composers, often nameless, worked within prescribed limits. A large body of the music centered around compositions for the mass, religious "feasts," and various holy days. These works, stylized in the early Middle Ages (c. 600-800) as so-called *plainsong* or *chant*,[5] evidenced an amazing degree of conformity to specific restrictions.

The chorestration of plainsong was confined to male voices singing in unison, with occasional solo introductions or interruptions. The vocal range of this monophonic style was limited to restricted intervallic leaps, and the tonal content of the melodies was strictly defined by certain modal scales acceptable to the church authorities. Set principles of rhythmical interpretation were handed down through the years, and the gradual development of two-, three-, and four-part (voice) styles—known as *organum*—did not emerge until the twelfth and thirteenth centuries.

Early expressions of harmony that featured the use of perfect fourths and fifths in parallel motion still exist. A three-part or four-part harmonic fabric was obtained by doubling these intervals at the octave. The result, of course, was a constant *coupling* of the melody in 3p or 4p.[6]

X. 1
a) Melody (chant-style)   (b) Melody with couplings

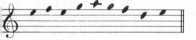 

Coupling, traditionally known as *parallel organum* (c. 900), gradually yielded to less rigid forms in which the plainsong melody was accompanied by one or more voices with a rhythmic structure of a generally contrasting nature—a rudimentary linear counterpoint. The principal types were *free* organum, *melismatic* organum and *measured* organum.

X. 2
a) Free organum (c. 1150; 1-4 attacks against 1)

(b) Melismatic organum (c. 1150; many attacks against 1)

(c) Measured organum (c. 1200; 2p, with specific rhythmic values,
     against 1p)

Even though other intervals were used, perfect fourth
and fifths continued to receive a great deal of emphasis.

Coupling, which was adopted in a general sense (as chord
in fourths and fifths) by rock groups in the 1960s, began it
resurgence as a significant technique in the early twentieth cen
tury. The following traditional examples are from the first quar
ter of the century.

EX. 3   Bartok, Fourteen Bagatelles, No. 11 (1908)
        (3p couplings, diatonic)

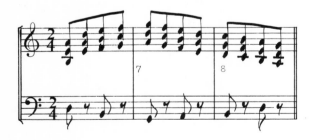

EX. 4 Debussy, <u>Engulfed Cathedral</u> (1910)
       (3p, 5p couplings in fourths and fifths)

EX. 5 Vaughn-Williams, Pastoral Symphony, I (1922)
       (3p, fourths and fifths over triadic couplings)

EX. 6 Respighi, <u>Pines of Rome</u>, II (1924)
    (7p couplings in fourths and fifths)

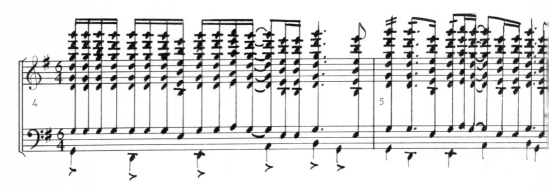

The Period of Renaissance Individualism
(Principal Musical Developments: Vocal Counterpoint and Tertian Harmony)

During the fourteenth and early fifteenth centuries (*c.* 1300-1450) the rigidity of the Middle Ages began to relax somewhat in preparation for the adventurous period of the Renaissance. Secular music in the form of ballades, rondeaux, and madrigals gained the attention of established composers; more animated and metrically complicated rhythmic patterns became standard fare; and unusual displacements of melodic/rhythmic relationships were featured in the *isorhythmic* motets of Guillaume de Machaut (d. 1377). In his work, the use of three-part harmony was also clearly established.[7] By about 1450 the gap between medievalism and the Renaissance had been bridged. Numerous changes in compositional tendencies and techniques attested to the fact that an era of individual experimentation had begun.

Composers, as individuals, began to exercise their influence over broad areas of scholarly activity. So much so that expressions such as the "school of Dufay," or the "school of Josquin" (des Prez) have become common. The use of four independent harmony parts was standardized, as was the consistent use of canonic imitation as a contrapuntal device. Ecclesiastical con-

trol over the content of liturgical music became so lax that secular texts frequently appeared in sacred compositions. Con-
versely, it was quite common to replace the words of a secular
chanson with religious words. There was also a lack of restriction on the interchanging of vocal and instrumental music. The
polyphonic chanson—the most important form of French and
Flemish vocal music in the early Renaissance—was transcribed
for lute and keyboard (note-for-note, with some added ornamentation where necessary) by the Italians, thus producing the instrumental *canzona*.

During the Renaissance, complete triads and their inver-
sions (in four parts) became standardized. And, although the
triad predominated as the harmonic basis for the linear counterpoint of the period, seventh chords were occasionally seen as the
result of passing tones, suspensions, and auxiliary tones that
occurred between the principal triadic structures. As early as
Dufay (d. 1474) it was quite common to encounter complete
four-part harmonic textures. The next example—from his mass,
Se la face ay pale[8]—even contains a secondary dominant in measure 8:

EX. 7 Kyrie

(Arrows indicate passing sevenths)

By the time of Josquin des Prez (d. 1521) it was clear that
a major period of polyphony was underway. The device of
canonic imitation became a prerequisite for knowledgeable
motet writing, and the four-to-eight-part textures were clearly
excellent models of vocal counterpoint. Still, the harmonic basis
(triads and implied seventh chords) for the masses, motets, and

madrigals of the period was quite clear, and remained so
through the time of Lassus and Palestrina (both d. 1594) in the
High Renaissance.

EX. 8 Josquin, <u>Ave Maria</u> (motet)

(Arrow indicates passing seventh; brackets indicate imitative
motives)

EX. 9 Palestrina, <u>Missa Papae Marcelli</u>

(a) Credo

(b) Credo

(c) Gloria

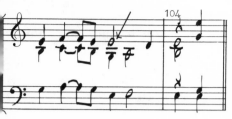

(Arrows indicate sevenths formed by suspension)

Ex. 10   Gesualdo (d. 1614), Moro Lasso (madrigal)

Arrows indicate sevenths)

The Period of Baroque Expansion
(Principal Musical-Harmonic Developments: Instrumental Counterpoint and Standardization of Triads/Sevenths)

The individualistic experiments of the Renaissance did not terminate with the advent of the Baroque period about 1600. They became, instead, the catalysts for an even more impressive period of expansion and growth.

During the latter part of the Renaissance, an interest in formal compositions for the solo voice received increased impetus due, probably, to practical problems related to the performance of madrigals. The Renaissance madrigal, usually written for five unaccompanied voices, could be more easily performed if fewer persons were needed for realization of the music. The problem was solved by assigning the principal melodic line to a solo voice and adapting the remaining voice parts for keyboard or lute. These solo madrigals, also referred to as *continuo* madrigals, were handled masterfully by composers such as Monteverdi; they prepared the way for a complete genre of solo songs by Caccini (d. 1618), known as *monodies*.[9] The importance of such publications can hardly be overestimated since they laid the practical foundations for *opera, oratorio,* and the *cantata.*

Many other forms also evolved and/or reached their high point in the Baroque. The *trio sonata*,[10] *suite, fugue, invention* and all of the forms stemming from the protestant *chorale* (chorale prelude, chorale motet, chorale fantasy, chorale cantata) were perfected by J.S. Bach and his contemporaries. Even the *symphony* had its origin in the Baroque *sinfonia* and operatic *overture.*

Solo works for a variety of instruments became extremely popular. Keyboard instruments (organ and harpsichord) assumed an important accompanimental role and were almost always present in small or large instrumental ensembles. The strong, harmony-defining left-hand part of the keyboard was normally doubled by a cello or member of the viol family. So constantly did this occur that the doubled left-hand part became known as the continuous bass, or *basso continuo.* As instrumental range and technique expanded, it was logical that the overall texture of the music would become rhythmically and melodically ornate (as the term "Baroque" suggests). Thus, the related techniques of embellishment and improvisation that developed during this time were established as standard procedures that affected all of the music to follow. Even today, the principal rules governing melodic ornamentation stem from Baroque practices and the period is rightfully regarded as the first era of improvisation.

The repetitive rhythms of the basso continuo are highly suggestive of the ostinato-like patterns of twentieth-century popular music: first as found in the "boogie-woogie" left-hand keyboard ostinatos of early jazz, and later in rhythm-and-blues and rock.

The predominating use of triads in the Renaissance gave way in the Baroque to the complete standardization of seventh chords. This process of change in harmonic development was enhanced after 1600 by the numerous lute and keyboard transcriptions to which the vocal compositions of the Renaissance had been subjected. Seventh chords, in the Baroque, became well established as independent entities. In the following examples the seventh chord is treated as a self-sufficient sonority:

EX. 11 Corelli (d. 1713), <u>Concerto Grosso No. 8</u>

EX. 12 J. S. Bach, <u>Chorale No. 262</u>

EX. 13   J. S. Bach, <u>The Well-Tempered Klavier</u>, Prelude No. 1

EX. 14   Haydn (d. 1809), <u>Symphony No. 101</u>, I

The Period of Classical Equilibrium
(Principal Musical-Harmonic Developments: Homophony and
   Standardization of Ninths)

The Baroque, for all of its innovations and multiple achievements, was also burdened with certain excesses and limitations. The ceaseless activity of the basso continuo plus the equally active treble voices often bordered on rhythmic saturation. Also, in spite of the abundance of melodic motives, there was very little extended development of themes, as such.

Motivic figures were prolifically displayed and complete themes were often stated, but specific and orderly extension of thematic material was rare. A better balance was needed between motives and thematic development; between rhythmically active bass/treble voices and relatively inactive inner parts; and between the intellectual and emotional content of the compositions. These improvements were supplied by the composers of the Classical period: Haydn, Mozart, Beethoven, and their contemporaries.

The problem of equal part activity was solved in the Classical period. Each "voice" in the orchestra played its own individual role within the overall texture. Solo and ensemble passages were nicely balanced. A predominant *homophonic melody* was clearly perceivable at all times, and significant segments of the principal themes were distributed among all of the instrumental choirs. A reasonable equality was achieved between harmonic and melodic elements—the development of the melody was clear, but one never lost interest in the primary and secondary harmonic objectives outlined by the chord progressions. And the controlled thematic units were skillfully deployed within the framework of specific forms such as the *rondo* and *sonata allegro*.

These forms, and others, emphasized the element of balance by means of the disposition of thematic recurrence. The rondo stressed the predictable return of the theme, separated by symmetrically spaced interludes of contrasting material. The sonata allegro was basically a three-part ABA form with optional introduction and coda. Within the first *A* section (exposition) the principal themes were stated, and they were restated in the final *A* section (recapitulation). The *B* section was reserved for the development of these themes. All of the motivic and thematic events were masterful examples of the art of transition, wherein melodic or harmonic activity grew out of previous statements and formed a series of *linear* occurrences leading to specific, clearly defined points of emphasis or cadence.

Careful control was also manifest in the handling of orchestral color. A balanced presentation of the various sections enabled the composer to maintain the desired objective of "unity in variety." Woodwinds, strings, and brass spoke alone as well as in combination. And all of the wind instruments—in contrast to the Baroque practice of nonstop performance—were allowed breathing space in order to sustain peak efficiency.

The period was a time of inspired restraint, disciplined emotion, intellectual fervor, and provocative aesthetic objectives. Its label—"Classical"—is an apt one. Of all the periods in the past thousand years of music history, it has best stood the test of analytical criticism by both artist and pedant.

Harmonically, the development of chord structures in the Classical period included the ninth as a frequently-seen sonority. The ninth chord, in its early stages (*e.g.* in the Baroque), developed very slowly—usually with careful preparation and resolution. Its evolution followed generally the same pattern as that of the seventh: first the preparation of tones that formed the interval of the ninth; later the use of the chord as an independent sonority. In many instances, the ninth degree appeared without preparation or as part of a chordal arpeggio, but in almost all cases it resolved stepwise, until its free and unrestricted use became common in the late Romantic period when textural sonority began to assume a more important role than harmonic function *per se*.

EX. 15   J. S. Bach, <u>Fantasie and Fugue</u>

EX. 16   Mozart (d. 1791), <u>Fantasia and Sonata No. 18</u>

EX. 17   Haydn, <u>Piano Sonata in D Major</u>, II

EX. 18   Beethoven (d. 1827)

(a) <u>Symphony No. 3</u>, I

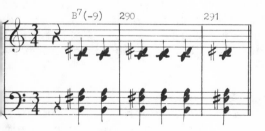

(b) <u>Leonora Overture No. 3</u>

The Period of Romantic Emotionalism
(Principal Harmonic Development: Sonority as a Device for Textural Control)

The closing years of the Classical period indicated that an artistic idiom emphasizing formal balance and equilibrium could not forever serve as an adequate means of personal expression for composers. A vast gap separated the precise punctuations and broken chords of the "Mannheim strings"[11] from the broad choral-orchestral panoramas of Beethoven's *Ninth Symphony*. The egoistic drives of genius composers, freed from royal and ecclesiastical domination, were struggling to surface. Beethoven, scorner of patrons, critics, and performers alike, had opened the way for exploitation of grandiose sentiments. His last symphonies, string quartets, and piano sonatas, which were written after he became deaf, were monuments to the free spirit. The "I" in music could no longer be denied and a cult of extremes took shape, wherein individual feeling was considered the ultimate criterion.

Within three years of Beethoven's death, Hector Berlioz produced his *Symphonie fantastique,* which depicts the hallucinatory adventures of a drug addict. The music was highly descriptive and adhered to a specific story. It was not the first example of program music, but it was easily the most influential; it clearly confirmed the break with Classicism. The tone poems of Liszt and Strauss, later in the century, were indebted to the Berlioz work; it also presaged the colorful orchestration that was to see full flower in the twentieth century. And, of course, the story-line of the *Fantastic Symphony* clearly indicated the departure from traditional subject material. Later would come the Liszt *Faust Symphony,* the Strauss *Death and Transfiguration* and *Till Eulenspiegel,* Rachmaninoff's *Isle of the Dead,* Debussy's *Prélude á l'Apres-midi d'un faune,* the Sibelius *En Saga,* and many other similar works.

Constant improvement in the quality of piano construction soon made virtuoso solo piano literature possible. Chopin created the concert étude—an example which was followed by Liszt, who wrote studies of "transcendental" difficulty *(Études d' exécution transcendante)*—and the nineteenth century saw the rise of a school of piano virtuosity that has not been surpassed. Pianists of legendary prowess concertized throughout the world, and in most cases they were the object of highly emotional adoration. The cult of ego-worship extended also into the world of opera, where Richard Wagner was able to demand the construction of an operatic center at Bayreuth for the performance of his works alone. The emotional fervor of Wagner's admirers was apparently undiminished by the length of some of his masterworks. The *Ring* cycle, for example, required over twelve hours to perform.

By contrast, certain Chopin preludes can be played in less than a minute. And the piano works in short forms of both Chopin and Schumann (known as "character pieces") were the opposite extreme of a production such as Mahler's *Symphony No. 8* (the "symphony of a thousand"). An unwillingness to submit to restrictions, a strong compulsion to paint egoistically either vast panoramas of sound or tightly concentrated distillations of supercharged emotion, and an inspired vision of the artist's role in society—all of these factors were influential in shaping the musical forces of the Romantic period.

The beginning of an expanded concept of harmonic function in the late nineteenth century was apparent in the continuing development of the ninth chord as an independent harmonic entity. The use of chords as the basis for accompaniment of homophonic melodies was gradually giving way to the treatment of sonority as a device for textural control. Chords of higher tension (ninths, elevenths, thirteenths) contain a unique, memorable quality due to their density and dissonant connotations. For this reason, they were ideal for the establishment of a sonorous fabric that could suggest a kind of harmonic "mood" and, as a consequence, the concern with linear development and continuity yielded to experimentation with rich, luxuriant masses of vertical sonority.

In some cases, the practice of resolving the ninth as a non-harmonic tone (Ex. 19) was continued, but by the early twentieth century its use as an unrestricted sonority was clearly established.

EX. 19 Schumann (d. 1856), Träumerei

EX. 20 Tchaikovsky (d. 1893), Romeo and Juliet

EX. 21 Brahms (d. 1897), _Intermezzo_, Op. 119, No. 1

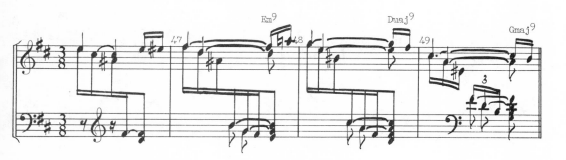

EX. 22 Debussy (d. 1918), _Children's Corner_, No. 3 (1908)

The employment of structural sonorities for the purpose of textural control became well established after the turn of the century and led to the widespread use of eleventh and thirteenth chords as well as ninths. In many cases, chords of greater dissonance began to appear as the result of embellishing basic seventh chord harmonies:

EX. 23 Wagner, <u>Tristan and Isolde</u>, Prelude (1859)

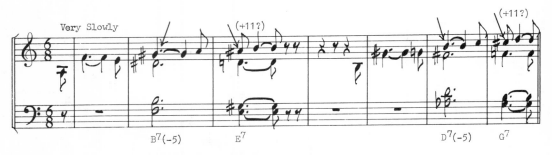

(Arrows indicate chromatic appoggiaturae and passing tones)

By the beginning of the twentieth century, the formation of ninths, elevenths, and thirteenths no longer required linear justification, and all of these structures functioned as independent, clearly defined sonorities.

EX. 24 Ravel, <u>String Quartet</u>, I (1903)

Reprinted by permission of International Music Company, publisher.

EX. 25   Scriabin, Désir (1908)

(a)

(b)

EX. 26   Ravel, Gaspard de la nuit, "Le Gibet" (1909)

EX. 27 Ravel, <u>Valses nobles et sentimentales</u>, No. 1 (1911)

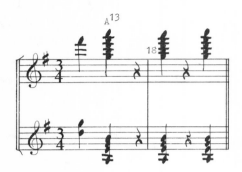

EX. 28 Debussy, <u>Six épigraphes antiques</u>, No. 4 (1915)

(a)   (b)

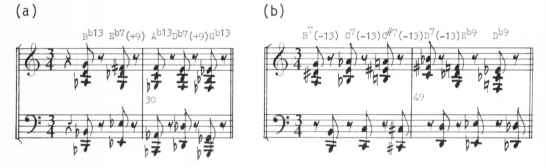

EX. 29   Debussy, <u>En blanc et noir</u>, III (1915)

EX. 30   Griffes, <u>Four Roman Sketches</u>, No. 1 (1916)

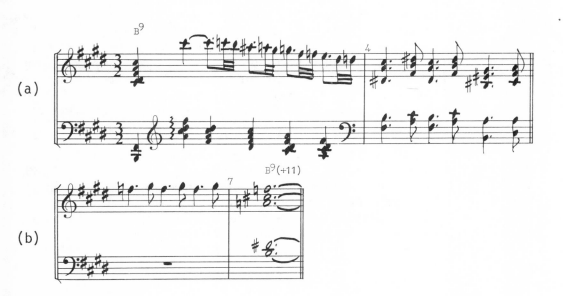

The Period of Twentieth-Century Reaction
(Principal Harmonic Developments: Tertian Superpositions,
   Non-Tertian Combinations)

Art from the Renaissance until the twentieth century was primarily concerned with progression in the general sense of the word—a smoothly connected, logical sequence of anticipated events.[12]. Perspective, specific objectives, and the connection of related ideas one to the other were outstanding factors in the visual arts and in music. Unity, continuity of line, and the arrangement of events in linear order predominanted, even in the Romantic period where a moratorium was declared on restraint. In spite of the predilection for extreme emotionalism, the Romantic composer was quite conscious of formal construction and the need for a sequential order between related sound-terms.

Music and art of the twentieth century, however, began the exploration of devices representing a sharp break with earlier procedures. Progression and smoothly connected ideas were rejected in favor of juxtaposition, superposition, simultaneity, and abruptness. Logical sequence was frequently replaced by disconnection and unexpectedness.

Music through the nineteenth century accomplished smooth transition by means of voice-leading, harmonic progression, and melodic development. Tones were organizationally related to each other or to a tonal center, and one moment was connected to the next. Contemporary music, by contrast, is frequently cut short without harmonic resolution, coda, or cadence; contrasting textures and scales are superposed to produce conflict; sudden register shifts and jagged melodic contours, scattered throughout a pointillistic fabric, replace specific meaning with ambiguity. In short, it is a reaction against everything traditional.

Several of the characteristics of early twentieth-century traditional works reappeared in the rock idiom of the 1960s. Unusual harmonic resolution (or the lack of resolution by means of the fade coda), evasive cadential patterns, and sudden contrasts in texture (timbre) through electronic means were common features of compositions in the rock period.

The twentieth century interest in psychoanalysis and self-searching was an important catalyst to the reactionary movement. The turn toward self-examination had already been stimulated in the nineteenth century by the French Symbolist poets. Mallarmé (d. 1898), Verlaine (d. 1896), Rimbaud (d. 1891), and Valéry (1871-1945) examined the workings of consciousness and the nature of creative thought. In Austria, the studies of Freud (1856-1939) and other Austro-Germans such as Jung, Adler, and Köhler laid the foundation of twentieth-century psychoanalytic practices. By 1914, Freud had been translated into French, and the concern with the inner self had secured a place in the aesthetic considerations of the time. The symbolist (impressionist) poets, with their emphasis on subtle impressions, moods, and dreams—in which, they believed, lay the heart of reality—were precursors of the movement toward psychological introspection, which is also typical of the rock medium.

Debussy's *Afternoon of a Faun* established a manner of expression where color was as important as line and motive, and where the strict imitation of external reality gave way to a slow "unfocusing" that permitted subjective interpolation. The blurring of tonal outlines was hastened by the gradual elimination of dominant harmony, which had previously furnished directional impetus toward the tonic as the central focus. The next step, after Debussy, was the elimination of the tonic altogether. Tonic harmony was first dispersed and relocated by numerous consecutive modulations. This rendered the attraction of a key center less clear, and eventually the original tonality was withheld to the point where it became nonexistent.

The final step, then, was to refrain from any tonal statement; this was the principal characteristic of atonal music as employed in Expressionism. The sharp focus of tonality and tonic-dominant relationships, finally yielded to the blur of atonality in which a stated continuum of tone materials (a *tone-row*) could be freely manipulated in accordance with the subjective designs of the composer. This technique was presented and successfully continued by Schönberg and his disciples, Webern and Berg. Schönberg's *Pierrot Lunaire* (1912) was highly innovative with its use of the speaking-voice (*sprechstimme*) as opposed to the traditional singing voice in definite pitch. The indefinite vocal inflections of *sprechstimme* provided the ideal medium for the ambiguity, distortion, and semihysterical intensity that characterized the early twentieth century expressionist movement and, later, the vocal renditions of many rock musicians.

The concern with ambiguity and self-searching was also expressed through means other than Expressionism. Textures of ingenuous diatonic simplicity and repetitive ostinato were used to reflect a childlike vision of the world. The principal representative of this technique was Erik Satie, who scattered facetious directions through his deceptively simple compositions, such as "take off your glasses," "with profound respect," and "like a nightingale with a toothache." The satire and ambiguity in his approach emphasized childlike wonder and spontaneity, and reaffirmed innocence of attitude and technique. The logic of the child, with its forthright honesty, permits an open, subjective contemplation uncluttered by sophisticated pretense. This same reflective concern for the inner self and its true values has had continued expression in twentieth century folk music, both traditional and rock-oriented. Also, Debussy and Ravel wrote suites for children,[13] and even the complex Stravinsky produced works of diatonic simplicity, as in his *Five Easy Pieces* (1917).

Stravinsky's principal contribution, however, was the establishment of a generative force in France sufficient to counter the rise of Expressionism in Vienna. In 1910 he wrote the *Firebird Suite,* in 1911, *Petrouchka,* and in 1913, *The Rite of Spring.* All of these works were object lessons in a virile conception of music but, as mentioned earlier, it was *The Rite of Spring* that startled the public with its rhythmic shocks, directness, and power. Stravinsky's handling of rhythmic ostinato—a primitivistic device for hundreds of years—was unique due to the use of mixed metrical patterns that caused a continual shifting of accent. Ostinato, by its monotonous repetition, assists in the delineation of various strata of activity one from the other, and acts as a kind of "fundamental line" against which ideas can be worked out in other parts of the musical structure.

This kind of separation—dividing the total texture into clearly defined layers, each with its own rhythmic and melodic integrity—formed the basis for other kinds of separation and diffusion. Separate scales were superposed (*polymodality*); separate streams of harmony were employed simultaneously (*polyharmony*); and often a third layer was set up in opposition to the outer polymodal or polyharmonic strata. Each of these techniques, used by Stravinsky, became standard fare (c. 1915-1925) in the works of other musicians writing in Paris, such as Milhaud and Honegger.[14]

Polyharmony, the superimposition of separate and clearly recognizable chords (usually a series of triads or sevenths) one upon the other, was the principal device for establishing two (occasionally three) clearly defined layers of chordal activity.

EX. 31

(a) Major triads in
    polyharmony

(b) Major sevenths in
    polyharmony

In some situations, each layer of chords was in a different key, and the combination of harmonies from various tonalities resulted in *polytonality*.

EX. 32

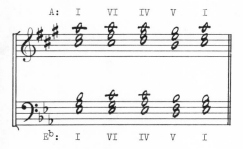

Some polyharmonic examples from traditional literature
include:

EX. 33 Stravinsky, <u>Le Sacre du Printemps</u>,
        "Danse des adolescentes" (1913)

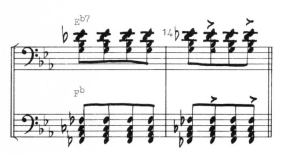

Copyright 1921 by Edition Russe de Musique. Copyright assigned
1947 to Boosey and Hawkes for all countries of the world. Reprinted by permission.

EX. 34 Koechlin, <u>Sonate pour piano et hautbois</u> (1915)

Reprinted by permission of Editions Salabert, Paris.

EX. 35 Milhaud, <u>The Libation Bearers</u>, III (1916)

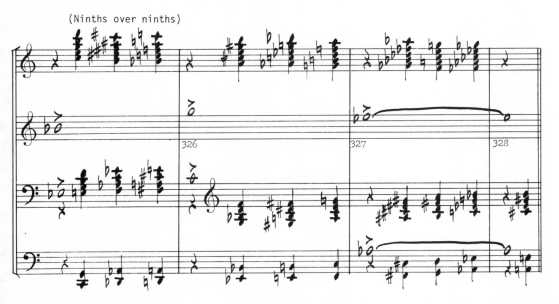

EX. 36 Ravel, <u>Concerto pour piano et orchestre</u>, III (1931)

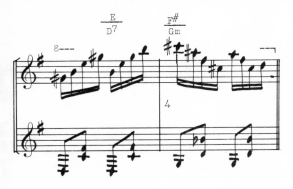

EX. 37   Honegger, <u>Symphony No. 5</u>, I (1950)

(Triads over triads)

Reprinted by permission of Editions Salabert, Paris.

Sometimes the "thickness" of each stratum was made overly obvious by using complete thirteenth chord structures. The following example should plainly illustrate what is meant by "textural sonority." Here, harmonic function is totally subservient to harmonic quality and texture, and the three layers of activity are clearly individualized.

EX. 38   Milhaud, <u>Les Euménides</u>, Act III (1922)

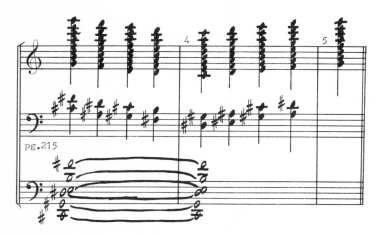

pg.215

Polychords were also used in canonic imitation:

EX. 39   Milhaud, <u>La déliverance de Thésée</u> (1927)

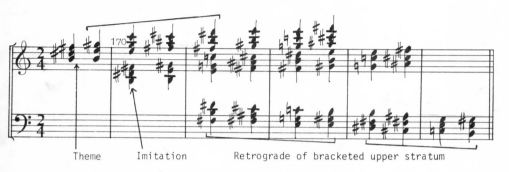

Theme   Imitation   Retrograde of bracketed upper stratum

At this point in time, Van Gogh's observation that "color
in itself expresses something, never mind the subject"[15] had become an established fact in the treatment of musical sonority[16].

Vertical intervallic arrangements are not limited to
structures in thirds. Chords in seconds, sevenths, fourths and
fifths also have been utilized to produce sonorities of very high
tension.

EX. 40   Honegger, <u>Horace Victorieux</u> (1921)—perfect fourths
         and augmented fourths

(a)

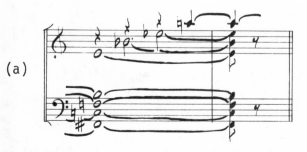

Honegger's *King David* (1921) also contains analogous situations (Section XVI, m.1-4; 10-14) where perfect fourths, and perfect and diminished fifths form structures of the following type:

(b)

EX. 41   Bartok, <u>Mikrokosmos</u> (1926-37)

(a) "Fourths"

(b) "Minor Seconds, Major Sevenths"

Other non-tertian intervallic combinations have been used that are the result of systems based upon particular scale sets. Principally, these include *pandiatonicism,* the *whole-step scale,* and the *chromatic scale* (as employed in *serial* technique).

Pandiatonicism—defined by Persichetti[17] as "combinations of any number of tones from the prevailing scale, placed in variable spacings"—is, specifically, the relation between a heterogeneous combination of pitch assemblages, often in superposition, whose structures (often unfamiliar) are restricted to a given scale.

EX. 42 Scale of C Major

The technique appears to have been popularized by Stravinsky, who employed it in *Petrouchka*.

EX. 43 Stravinsky, <u>Petrouchka</u>, I (1911)
        "Danse Russe" (Scale of C Major)

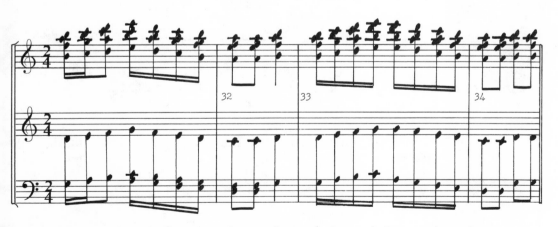

The whole-step (so-called "whole-tone") scale consists of six equal subdivisions of the octave. There are two possibilities:

EX. 44

All other combinations are but enharmonic variants of these two sets. Several of Debussy's compositions make sporadic use of the scale. The following example is from a work that is almost completely derived from whole-step intervals:[18]

EX. 45 Debussy, "Sails," Twelve Preludes, Book I (1910)

The same technique has been used occasionally by numerous twentieth century composers. Here is an example from Bartók:

EX. 46   Bartók, "Whole-Tone Scale," <u>Mikrokosmos</u> (1926-37)

Copyright 1940 by Hawkes and Son (London) Ltd.; renewed 1967.
Reprinted by permission of Boosey and Hawkes, Inc.

The chromatic scale forms the basis of serial *(or atonal)* technique, in which the twelve available tones are arranged in a series known as a *tone-row*. This procedure—originated by Schönberg during the first quarter of the twentieth century—has been widely explored by many composers; numerous papers and articles have been written that analyze and experiment with several variants of the original concept. Basically, the concern is with a pre-set order of twelve tones that serves as the model for melodic and harmonic combinations. The tone-row should not outline familiar tertian harmonies nor suggest tonality through melodic interval arrangement. The order of the series should remain unchanged (but see example below) throughout the composition, although it may be used in retrograde, inversion, and retrograde inversion. By superposing selected sets of tones from the tone-row, one can construct a large variety of atonal structures.[19]

EX. 47   Schönberg, <u>Suite für Klavier</u>, Op. 25 (1925)
         "Menuett"

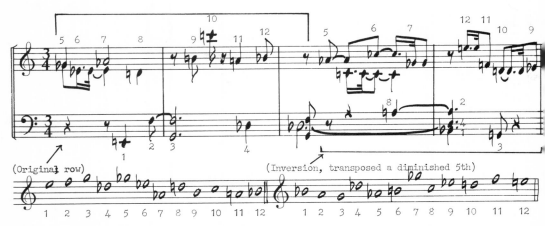

Used by permission of Belmont Music Publishers, Los Angeles, CA   9(
Copyright 1925 by Universal Edition. Copyright renewed 1952 by Ge
Schönberg.

EX. 48   Riegger, <u>Symphony No. 3</u>, I (1947)

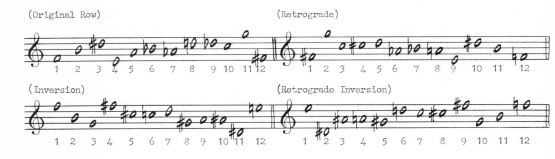

Ex. 48 (continued)

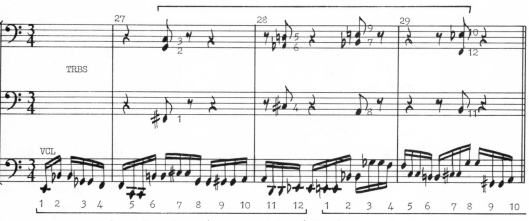

Harmony from retrograde position of row

TRBS

VCL

Inversion of row (transposed down ½ step)

These composers and their devices were part of the early twentieth-century movement toward almost total divisionism, diffraction, and dispersion.

It is significant that twentieth-century studies for the piano are often a study of individual elements. Bartók and Riegger, in sharp contrast to Chopin and other nineteenth-century masters, devoted complete pieces to the study of specific intervals and devices. Numerous examples of this occur in the *Mikrokosmos* of Bartók, and Riegger's *New and Old* includes such titles as "Major Second," "The Tritone," "Fourths and Fifths," etc. The emphasis toward divisionism led also to an interest in the nature of space, as such. Space, normally treated as the distance between events, became an event in itself—a tangible continuum to be worked around and within. The pointillistic formats of Seurat and other early twentieth-century painters had their counterpart in the scattered note placement and instrumental timbres of Webern.[20] The technique was later carried to further extremes by Karlheinz Stockhausen, and other sound-experimenters such as John Cage set up long periods of silence within which occasional pitches were inter-jected without pre-set planning ("indeterminacy"). Even Var-èse's *Ionisation* (1931) essentially ignored pitch by using percus-sive instruments of indeterminate pitch. The large orchestras of the nineteenth century spread before the listener a broad, mac-roscopic palette. Twentieth century ensembles microscopically dissected the elements of music and frequently they produced abstract textures that provided only a minimum rate of informa-tion exchange.

Further experiments in textural sonority are still in prog-ress. The advent of the electronic medium has provided the most important means for manipulation of sonorous phenomena, and it is likely that this area of experimentation will continue to receive prime attention for a considerable period. The develop-ment of chord structures, as such, reached its peak during the era of polyharmonic superposition and atonality; thus it is not surprising to witness a regression from structural complexity (in folk and rock music) during the third quarter of this century.

The harmony of rock is an example of the resurgence of an ingenuous approach to musical expression. A review of the selected rock-styled progressions in Part II and III will reveal a generally unsophisticated harmonic vocabulary but, neverthe-less, a specific and clearly defined collection of techniques that lend themselves to duplication and application.

Generally, the musical events that occurred during the rock period may be regarded as a capsulation of a variety of trends and concepts that have existed throughout the last few centuries of musical development in Western civilization. Some of the more obvious correlations are:

Harmonies of open fourths and fifths	Pre-tertian period of organum
Irregular sectional form and order of thematic recurrences; ambiguity of key signature; melodic modal influences; folk influences	Medieval, Renaissance periods
Emphasis on low tension (triadic) structures and chord-degree harmonization (as opposed to realization of a given bass); resurgence of chanson-like, madrigalian vocal settings	Renaissance period
Secondary dominants; dominant minor; subdominant cadences; chordal modal interchange	Renaissance, Baroque periods
Diatonic/mixed-diatonic harmony	Renaissance, Baroque, Classical periods
Chromatic Harmony	Romantic period
Symmetric harmony; neo-expressionism (syllabic, dynamic, and semantic distortion); neo-primitivism (ostinato, phrasic repetition, low chord density-in-time)	Early Twentieth-Century period

Footnotes to Part I

[1]George T. Jones, *Symbols Used in Musical Analysis* (Catholic University of America. Published by Cooperative Research Program of the Office of Education, U.S. Dept. of HEW, 1964).

[2]Joseph Schillinger, *The Schillinger System of Musical Composition,* Vol. I (New York: Carl Fischer, 1941), p. 654.

[3]See historical reference materials in the Appendix, Section II, for a more complete description of the development of chord structures.

[4]The traditional expression "chord of the sixth" (triad in first inversion) will not be used. A triad with the third as its lowest tone will always be designated as a $^6_3$ chord in order to avoid confusion with the common "added sixth" chord of contemporary music. The triad C with third in the bass may be referred to as C^6_3 , but never as C_6 which, regardless of inversion, means

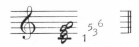

[5]W. W. Austin, *Music in the Twentieth Century* (New York: Norton, 1966), p. 269.

[6]Austin, *Music in the Twentieth Century,* p. 270.

[7]The same type of structure is the first sonority in Debussy's *Afternoon of a Faun*; therefore, might it not also be termed the "Debussy Chord" or even the "Faun" chord?

[8]As defined in Glareanus' work, *Dodecachordon* (1547), in which all of the traditionally used modes are noted. The Locrian mode, however, is not included.

[9]The medieval use of "Greek" modes actually involves little more than a cursory adaptation of some of the names attached to a limited number of Greek scales. See the *Musurgia* recording series, "The Theory of Classical Greek Music," for an actual laboratory duplication of the ancient Greek modes.

[10]*Gymnopédie No. 1* has been subjected to variations and recorded by Blood, Sweat & Tears as *Variations on a Theme by Erik Satie.*

[11]Compare Bert Konowitz, *The Complete Rock Piano Method* (New York: Alfred Music, 1972), p. 16, and Frank Metis, *Rock Modes & Moods* (New York: Marks Music, 1970), pp. 4, 18.

Konowitz uses the six-tone blues scale:

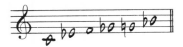

The Metis scale has seven tones:

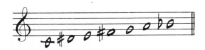

Footnotes to Part II

[1]See entry at "Cadence" in the *Harvard Dictionary of Music,* 2nd Ed. (Cambridge: Belknap Press, 1970).

[2]Compare Adele Katz, *Challenge to Music Tradition* (New York: DaCapo Press, 1972) and Felix Salzer, *Structural Hearing* (New York: Dover Publications, 1962), for excellent analyses of Schenker's theories.

[3]Schillinger, *The Schillinger System of Musical Composition,* p. 386.

[4]Richard Bobbitt, "The Physical Basis of Intervallic Quality," *Yale Journal of Music Theory,* November 1959.

Footnotes to the Appendix

[1]Album Notes by Paul Nelson for *We Are The Doors.* (New York: Music Sales Corp., 1968).

[2]Nelson, *We Are The Doors.*

[3]Bertram Konowitz, *Music in Modern American Society* (Albany: University of the State of New York, 1971), p. 2.

[4]A rather frequent exception to this is the dominant seventh with raised ninth, which appears in most soul rock.

[5]See Willi Apel, *Gregorian Chant* (Bloomington: Indiana University Press, 1958).

[6]The letter *p*, throughout this study, stands for *part*. Coupling in 3p, therefore, refers to coupling in three parts. The given melody is always included as one of the parts.

[7]In the *Notre Dame Mass*: probably the first complete polyphonic setting of a mass by a single composer.

[8]Transcription of the complete first movement given by Carl Parrish and J.F. Ohl, *Masterpieces of Music Before 1750* (New York: Norton, 1951), p. 43.

[9]The *Nuove Musiche* of 1602.

[10]Actually for four instruments—two treble instruments, keyboard, and cello—but the keyboard player and cellist read from the same part, so the work could be performed by three players, even though the cellist might be absent.

[11]Featured with the Mannheim orchestra (*c.* 1750), under Johann Stamitz) which played an important part in the development of the early Viennese classical style.

[12]For an interesting comparison of the arts of transition *vs* juxtaposition, see Roger Shattuck, *The Banquet Years* (New York: Doubleday, 1961), p. 332 ff.

[13]*The Children's Corner* and *Ma mère l'oye*

[14]Richard Bobbitt, "The Harmonic Idiom in the Works of 'Les Six'" (Ph.D. dissertation, Boston University, 1963). p. 162 ff.; p. 259 ff.

[15]Maurice Raynal, *Modern Painting* (Geneva: Skira, 1953), p. 66.

[16]The gradual development of chord structures from triads to sevenths to ninths, elevenths, and thirteenths should not be confused with the popular fallacy that such development is in accord with the overtone series. The harmonic series corresponds only *approximately* to *one* of the thirty-six available master structures, and there are, of course, thirty-five additional master structures which have no similarity to the natural harmonic series.

(Overtones of fundamental C₂)

(Approximation
master structur

[Tones with minus signs not compatible with actual pitches in just (natural) intonation.]

[17]Vincent Persichetti, *Twentieth Century Harmony* (New York: Norton, 1961), p. 223.

[18]There are a few chromatic passing tones, and a brief change of modality occurs in the G-flat pentatonic scale.

[19]See the *Harvard Dictionary of Music* (2nd Ed., p. 766) and other standard reference sources for detailed descriptions of serial techniques.

[20]Anton Webern, *Sechs Bagatellen für Streichquartett* (1913).

Glossary

AREA PROLONGATION (Harmonic): Activating, or filling in, the intervallic space between *root* tones of principal importance in a given tonal area. Traditional harmonic area prolongation usually fills in the space between tonic-dominant roots or tonic-subdominant roots. The added tones may become the source of new chords (Part II, Chap. 6).

AREA PROLONGATION (Melodic): Activating, or filling in, the intervallic space between *melodic* tones of principal importance in a given tonal area. Traditional melodic area prolongation usually fills in the space between tones of the tonic triad, or dominant triad, or subdominant triad. The added tones may become the source of new chords (Part II, Chap. 6).

BASSO CONTINUO: "Continuous bass." A clearly defined, rhythmically active bass line; usually given prominence by doubling the left-hand of a keyboard part with electric or acoustic bass. The continuous bass is often repetitive and frequently forms ostinato patterns, as in the left-hand of early jazz "boogie-woogie" piano music.

BLUES SCALE: The scale that results when a lowered third, lowered fifth, and lowered seventh are added to a major scale. The added, lowered, tones may be used in place of, or juxtaposed with, the unaltered third, fifth, or seventh (Part I, Chap. 5).

CADENCE (Harmonic): A chord progression that points toward, or delineates, a tonal center or "tonic-like" area. The tonal center may be temporary or (relatively) permanent (Part II, Chap. 6).

CANONIC IMITATION: The literal, imitative-repetition of a melodic figure, motive, or phrase. The imitation may be at any interval; traditionally the repetition is at the interval of an octave (or unison), perfect fifth, or perfect fourth.

CANTATA: A Baroque compositional form combining solo songs (arias), choral sections, and instrumental interludes.

CHANSON: The French word for song. Early songs, or *canzonas* (Italian), were accompanied contrapuntally (with as many as four parts, total) rather than with chords.

CHANT: Plainsong. The monophonic, liturgical music of the Roman church. Chant melodies were normally restricted to one of the ecclesiastical modes: Dorian, Phrygian, etc. (Appendix, Section II.)

CHORALE: A harmonized hymn-tune for congregational singing in the Protestant church.

CHORESTRATION: Scoring for choral groups; the counter-part of orchestration. Orchestration transcribes and adapts music (usually piano compositions) for orchestral use. Chorestration transcribes music for choral use.

CHORD-DEGREE HARMONIZATION: The assignment of variable chord-degrees (root, or third, or fifth in rock harmony) to the same tone or different tones. Each tone is then harmonized with a major or minor triad (Part I, Chap. 3).

CHORDAL DENSITY-IN-TIME: A "measure" of chordal quantity. The total number of individual chords per section of a composition, or the total number of chords in the entire work (Part II, Chap. 11).

CHROMATIC GROUPS: A progression of (usually) three chords resulting from the assignment of chord-degrees to adjacent tones linked by half-step (Part I, Chap. 2).

CHROMATIC HARMONY: Chord progression based on chromatic groups.

CHROMATIC SCALE: A scale of consecutive half-steps; usually containing twelve tones.

CONTINUO MADRIGAL: A Renaissance madrigal (poetic vocal music) transcribed from the usual setting of five unaccompanied voices to one of solo voice plus keyboard or lute. The strong, progression-defining bass line accounts for the name "continuo."

COUPLING: The addition of one or more tones in similar or parallel motion to a given pitch sequence. Tones or chords may be coupled at any interval below or above. Types: diatonic, constant, or variable.

CYCLE (Negative): Root motion, between two different chords, in *upward* (including octave adjustments) movement of thirds, fifths, or sevenths (Part II, Chap. 7).

CYCLE (Positive): Root motion, between two different chords, in *downward* (including octave adjustments) movement of thirds, fifths, or sevenths (Part II, Chap. 7).

DECEPTIVE CADENCE: Replacing an anticipated tonic (or tonic-like) chord with a substitute for the tonic (Part II, Chap. 8).

DIATONIC HARMONY: Harmonic progression where chord roots and upper structures belong to the same scale (Part I, Chap. 2).

EXPANSION: The distribution of the tones of a scale in open form (Part I, Chap. 1).

EXPRESSIONISM: A movement in painting and music that relied upon caricature and distortion to parody reality. It achieved its effect through exaggerated emphasis.

FADE CODA: A coda where the player is directed to "Repeat and Fade"; to play the final two or four measures over and over, and softer with each repetition, until the music becomes inaudible (Part II, Chap. 8).

FIGURED BASS: A Baroque system of chord notation. Numbers written beneath each bass tone indicate the intervals to be added above a particular tone. Realization of each interval combination outlines the chord of the moment.

FRENCH SIX: One of three (French, German, Italian) dominant seventh-type chord structures built on the lowered sixth degree of the major scale. The actual tones are root, third, lowered fifth, and augmented sixth. In isolation, the sonority corresponds enharmonically to a dominant seventh, lowered fifth. It resolves normally to V of the key.

FUGUE: A contrapuntal composition employing discontinuous canonic imitation; canonic passages separated by modulatory interludes (episodes).

GERMAN SIX: One of three (French, German, Italian) dominant seventh-type chord structures built on the lowered sixth degree of the major scale. The actual tones are root, third, fifth, and augmented sixth. In isolation, the sonority corresponds enharmonically to a dominant seventh. It resolves normally to I of the key.

HOMOPHONIC MELODY: A single-line melody supported by chordal accompaniment.

IMPRESSIONISM: A movement (c. 1880-1920) in painting and music that relied upon texture and the "impression" of color and structure as opposed to dependence on linear symmetry and perspective.

INCOMPLETE TRIAD: A triad without the third. Actually it is a misnomer, since all triads must have three different tones.

INTERVALLIC SYMMETRY (Root Motion): Non-diatonic root patterns that follow a specific plan of numerical distribution. Such patterns are the basis for symmetric harmony (Part I, Chap. 2).

INVENTION: A contrapuntal keyboard composition in two parts or three parts that corresponds generally to the fugue; it features canonic sections separated by interludes.

ISORHYTHM: "The same" rhythm. Repetition of the same rhythmic pattern against a pitch sequence, the total duration of which does *not* correspond to the total duration of the rhythmic phrase. The melody, therefore, is continually displaced against the set pattern of repeating rhythm.

ITALIAN SIX: One of three (French, German, Italian) dominant seventh-type chord structures built on the lowered sixth degree of the major scale. The sonority corresponds enharmonically to a dominant seventh with doubled third. It resolves normally to I of the key.

MASTER STRUCTURE (MS): The vertical sonority resulting from expansion of a complete chord scale (Part I, Chap. 1).

MELODIC AXIS: The principal tone center of a melodic figure, phrase, or section.

MIXED-DIATONIC HARMONY: Harmonic progression where chord roots belong to a specific scale, but the chord structures above the roots are not restricted to that scale (Part I, Chap. 2).

MODAL INTERCHANGE (Chordal): The alternation or exchange of any major harmony with the minor harmony on the same root (Part I, Chap. 5; Part II, Chap. 6 Summary/ Addenda; Part II, Chap. 9).

MODAL INTERCHANGE (Melodic): The alternation or exchange between a tone of an established scale and its own chromatic modification (Part I, Chap. 5).

MODAL MODULATION (Transition): The establishment of a new scale by introducing and retaining accidentals foreign to the original scale (Part I, Chap. 5).

MODE: Any pitch scale. Traditionally, any seven-unit scale whose intervals correspond to those found in the ecclesiastical modes (Part I, Chap. 5).

MONODY: Early Baroque term for a solo song in the declamatory style of very early opera (Appendix, Section II).

NEAPOLITAN SIXTH: A major triad constructed on the lowered second degree of a major or minor scale. Usually scored with the third of the chord in the bass (in the so-called "sixth" position).

OSTINATO: A continuously repeated figure or motive. An ostinato simply repeats a rhythmic pattern over and over, or it may also include literal repetition of the same pitches.

ORGANUM: Most commonly, the addition of an intervallic coupling in perfect fourths or fifths to a given pitch sequence. The strict coupling process of the Middle Ages, known as "strict" or "parallel" organum, gradually changed into less rigid forms such as "free," "melismatic," and "measured" organum (Appendix, Section II).

OVERTURE: Generally, a one-movement instrumental piece written as an introduction to an opera or oratorio.

PANDIATONICISM: A mixed combination of pitch assemblages, usually in superposition. The resulting heterogeneous structures are restricted to a given scale (Appendix, Section II).

PLAINSONG: Another term for *chant*.

POLYHARMONY (Polychord): The superposition of different, recognizable chord structures, such as: D major over C minor, or E maj. 7 over D maj. 7, etc.

POLYMODALITY: The superposition of melodies, each of which is recognizable as being in a different, clearly established, mode (Appendix, Section II).

POLYPHONY: Counterpoint. Two or more simultaneous melodies. If the melodies are in different modes, the result is polymodal polyphony.

POLYTONALITY: The superposition of two or more melodic or harmonic strata, each of which belongs to a clearly established major or minor key.

PRIMITIVISM: Concern with the characteristics of primitive cultures. Emphasis on simplicity of line, continuous repetition of ideas, overlays of rhythmic design, and the use of folk influences and traditions (Appendix, Section I).

RAISED SUBMEDIANT: The diminished seventh chord constructed on the raised sixth degree of the major scale. Normally resolves to V.

RAISED SUPERTONIC: The diminished seventh chord constructed on the raised second degree of the major scale. Normally resolves to I.

RONDO: A compositional form where a theme (with or without variations) is repeated continually, each restatement being separated by an interlude of contrasting material (Appendix, Section II).

SECONDARY DOMINANT: Any major triad or dominant seventh whose root moves *down* a perfect fifth to the root of the next chord. The triad or dominant seventh may *not,* however, be constructed on the fifth degree of the key of the moment (Part II, Chap. 7, Chap. 9).

SECONDARY SUBDOMINANT: Any major triad or dominant seventh whose root moves *up* a perfect fifth to the root of the next chord. The triad or dominant seventh may *not,* however, be constructed on the fourth degree of the key of the moment (Part II, Chap. 7).

SECONDARY SUBDOMINANT CHAIN: A continuous series of secondary subdominants.

SERIAL (Atonal) COMPOSITION: A compositional technique that avoids chord progressions, chord structures, or melodic figures that outline a key or conventional tonality. The twelve tones of the chromatic scale are the usual tone materials used for serial writing.

SINFONIA: An introductory instrumental piece. The term was popularized in the Baroque period and later affected the development of the term "symphony."

SONATA ALLEGRO: A compositional form, basically of three parts (*ABA*) with optional introduction and coda. Principal themes of the *A* section are developed in *B* and recapitulated in the final *A* section (Appendix, Section II).

SOUND-TERM: Any one of the several fundamental elements that make up a musical statement. A chord is the principal element or sound-term of harmonic progression; intervallic combinations are the essential sound-terms of melody; periodicity and attack are the principal sound-terms of rhythm.

STRUCTURAL SYMMETRY: Maintaining a fixed pattern of upper structures in a chord progression, regardless of the root movement (Part I, Chap. 2).

SUBSTITUTE CHORD: A chord structure that can take the place of another chord and functionally replace that chord in a progression (Part I, Chap. 4).

SUITE: A compositional form of the Baroque period made up of a series of dance movements. Each dance movement is of contrasting material; usually with a different time signature and/or tempo.

SUSPENDED FOURTH (*Sus 4*): In popular, professional music, a chord in which the fourth degree above the chord root is used in place of the third of the chord (Part II, Chap. 10).

SYMPHONY: The principal orchestral compositional form of the Classical period. The classical symphony depended primarily on an opening movement of the sonata allegro form plus two or three additional movements. Outstanding examples are the symphonies of Haydn, Mozart, and Beethoven.

SYMMETRIC HARMONY: Harmonic progressions whose chord roots and/or upper structures are based upon patterns of intervallic or structural symmetry, respectively.

TENSION: The intervallic relation between the top note of a chord structure and the chord root. The tension level of structures in thirds normally ranges from 1 to 13.

TERTIAN HARMONY: Chords constructed in intervals of thirds.

TIERCE DE PICARDIE: Ending a progression in a *minor* tonality with a *major* chord. The minor third of the final, tonic chord is changed to a major third. This is an early form of chordal modal interchange (Part I, Chap. 5).

TONE ROW: A preset, non-diatonic series of pitches used in serial, atonal composition.

TRIO SONATA: The most important instrumental form of the Baroque. It is scored for four players—two treble instruments plus keyboard and a low string instrument—but the latter two players read from the same part with the string instrument (cello or bass) doubling the left hand of the keyboard. The composition itself is a series of movements in contrasting tempo.

TROUBADOUR-TROUVÈRE SONGS: Solo songs (secular) of the Middle Ages. Sung by troubadours (Southern France) and trouvères (Northern France).

WHOLE-STEP SCALE: A symmetric pitch scale with the interval of one whole-step between each tone. Commonly called "whole-tone" scale.

Bibliography

Rock Compositions (Listed According to Performing Group)

THE ASSOCIATION

"Never My Love," D. Addrisi, Tamerlane Music (1967)

THE BEATLES

"Act Naturally," Morrison-Russell, Blue Book Music (1963)
"A Day in the Life," Lennon-McCartney, Northern Songs (1967)
"All My Loving," Lennon-McCartney, Northern Songs (1963)
"All Things Must Pass," G. Harrison, Harrisongs Music (1969)
"Awaiting on You All," G. Harrison, Harrisongs Music (1970)
"Bad Boy," Larry Williams, Venice Music (1965)
"Blue Jay Way," G. Harrison, Harrisongs Music (1967)
"Come Together," Lennon-McCartney, Northern Songs (1969)

"Eleanor Rigby," Lennon-McCartney, Northern Songs (1966)

"Good Day Sunshine," Lennon-McCartney, Northern Songs (1966)

"Here Comes the Sun," G. Harrison, Harrisongs Music (1969)

"Here, There, and Everywhere," Lennon-McCartney, Northern Songs (1966)

"Hey Jude," Lennon-McCartney, Northern Songs (1968)

"I'd Have You Anytime," Dylan-Harrison, Harrisongs Music (1970)

"I Feel Fine," Lennon-McCartney, Northern Songs (1964)

"If I Fell," Lennon-McCartney, Northern Songs (1964)

"I Me Mine," G. Harrison, Harrisongs Music (1970)

"I'm Happy Just to Dance with You," Lennon-McCartney, Northern Songs (1964)

"I Wanna Be Your Man," Lennon-McCartney, Northern Songs (1964)

"I Want to Hold Your Hand," Lennon-McCartney, Northern Songs (1963)

"Nowhere Man," Lennon-McCartney, Northern Songs (1965)

"Run of the Mill," G. Harrison, Harrisongs Music (1970)

"She Said She Said," Lennon-McCartney, Northern Songs (1969)

"Something," G. Harrison, Harrisongs Music (1969)

"Things We Said Today," Lennon-McCartney, Northern Songs (1964)

"Ticket to Ride," Lennon-McCartney, Northern Songs (1965)

"What is Life," G. Harrison, Harrisongs Music (1970)

"Yellow Submarine," Lennon-McCartney, Northern Songs (1966)

"Yesterday," Lennon-McCartney, Northern Songs (1965)

"You're Going to Lose That Girl," Lennon-McCartney, Northern Songs (1965)

THE BEE-GEES (All songs by Gibb-Gibb, Abigail Music.)

"Down to Earth," (1968)

"I Can't See Nobody," (1967)

"Idea," (1968)

"Indian Gin and Whiskey Dry," (1968)

"In the Summer of His Years," (1968)

"I've Got to Get a Message to You," (1968)

"Kilburn Towers," (1968)

"Let There Be Love," (1968)

"One Minute Woman," (1967)

BLOOD, SWEAT AND TEARS

"Forty Thousand Headmen," Winwood-Capaldi, Irving Music (1969)
"High on the Mountain," S. Katz, Blackwood Music (1969)
"Lucretia MacEvil," C. Thomas, Blackwood Music (1970)
"Mama Gets High," Bargeron-Katz, Blackwood Music (1968)
"Redemption," C. Thomas-Halligan, Blackwood Music (1968)
"Sometimes in Winter," S. Katz, Blackwood Music (1968)
"Spinning Wheel," C. Thomas, Blackwood Music (1969)
"The Battle," Katz-Halligan, Blackwood Music (1970)
"Variations on a Theme by Erik Satie," Blackwood Music (1968)

BRASIL 66

"Canto Triste," Lobo-Demoraes, Rodra Music (1968)
"Festa," Caymmi-Mota, Rodra Music (1968)
"So Many Stars," S. Mendez, Berna Music (1968)

JAMES BROWN
(All songs by James Brown, Dynatone Pub. Co.)

"Bring It Up," (1967)
"I'll Go Crazy," (1968)
"Papa's Got a Brand New Bag," (1965)
"Tell Me What You're Gonna Do," (1967)

BURT BACHARACH (All songs by Bacharach-David)

"As Long As There's An Apple Tree," Blue Seas-Jac Music (1967)
"Do You Know the Way to San Jose," Blue Seas-Jac Music (1967)
"Promises, Promises," Blue Seas-Jac Music (1968)
"Raindrops Keep Falling," Blue Seas-Jac Music (1969)
"The Forgotten Man," Arch (Schroeder) Music (1962)
"The Look of Love," Blue Seas-Jac Music (1967)
"This Guy's in Love with You," Blue Seas-Jac Music (1968)
"What the World Needs Now," Blue Seas-Jac (1965)

THE CARPENTERS

"We've Only Just Begun," Williams-Nichols, Irving Music (1970)

CREAM

"After Midnight," J. Cale, Viva Music (1966)
"Badge," Clapton-Harrison, Casserole Music (1969)
"Cat's Squirrel," S. Splurge, Casserole Music (1967)
"Don't Know Why," Bramlett-Clapton, Cotillion Music (1970)
"I've Told You for the Last Time," Cropper-Bramlett, Cotillion Music (1970)
"Let It Rain," Bramlett-Clapton, Cotillion Music (1970)
"Lovin' You, Lovin' Me," Bramlett-Clapton, Cotillion Music (1970)
"Sunshine of Your Love," Bruce-Brown-Clapton, Casserole Music (1968)
"Tales of Brave Ulysses," Clapton-Sharp, Casserole Music (1968)

CHICAGO (All music published by Aurelius Music.)

"Beginnings," R. Lamm (1969)
"Colour My World," Winwood-Miller (1970)
"Does Anybody Really Know What Time It Is," R. Lamm (1969)
"I'm A Man," Winwood-Miller (1966)
"In the Country," T. Kath (1970)
"Liberation," J. Pankow (1969)
"Listen," R. Lamm (1969)
"Movin' In," J. Pankow (1970)
"Prelude," Kath-Matz (1970)
"So Much to Say, So Much to Give," J. Pankow (1970)
"The Road," T. Kath (1970)
"To Be Free," J. Pankow (1970)
"West Virginia Fantasies," J. Pankow (1970)

CREEDENCE CLEARWATER
(All songs by J. Fogerty, Jondora Music.)

"Bad Moon Rising," (1969)
"Bootleg," (1969)
"Chameleon," (1970)
"Effigy," (1969)
"Feelin' Blue," (1969)
"Fortunate Son," (1969)
"Green River," (1969)
"Hideaway," (1970)
"It's Just a Thought," (1970)
"Poorboy Shuffle," (1969)
"Sinister Purpose," (1969)
"Who'll Stop the Rain," (1969)

CROSBY, STILLS, NASH & YOUNG

"Country Girl," N. Young, Cotillion/Broken Arrow Music (1970)
"Cut My Hair," D. Crosby, Guerilla Music (1970)
"Deja Vu," D. Crosby, Guerilla Music (1970)
"Forty-Nine Bye-Byes," S. Stills, Gold Hill Music (1969)
"Helplessly Hoping," S. Stills, Gold Hill Music (1969)
"Lady of the Island," G. Nash, Giving Room Music (1969)
"Teach Your Children," G. Nash, Giving Room Music (1970)
"You Don't Have to Cry," S. Stills, Gold Hill Music (1969)

THE DOORS
(Individual composers not listed; all songs published by Nipper
    Music.)

"Five to One," (1969)
"I Can't See Your Face," (1967)
"Love Street," (1968)
"Strange Days," (1967)
"Summer's Almost Gone," (1968)
"The Crystal Ship," (1967)
"The End," (1967)
"The Unknown Soldier," (1967)
"When the Music's Over," (1967)
"Wintertime Love," (1968)
"Yes, the River Knows," (1968)
"You're Lost, Little Girl," (1967)

BOB DYLAN (All songs by Bob Dylan.)

"All Along the Watchtower," Dwarf Music (1968)
"Ballad of Hollis Brown," M. Witmark & Sons (1963)
"Blowin' in the Wind," M. Witmark & Sons (1962)
"Like a Rolling Stone," M. Witmark & Sons (1965)
"Masters of War," N. Witmark & Sons (1963)

JACKSON FIVE

"Never Can Say Goodbye," C. Davis, Jobete Music (1970)

JIMI HENDRIX
(All songs by Jimi Hendrix, Sea Lark-Yameta.)

"Castles Made of Sand," (1968)
"Fifty-First Anniversary," (1968)

"Little Wing," (1968)
"Moon, Turn the Tides," (1968)
"Nineteen Eighty-Three," (1968)
"One Rainy Wish," (1968)
"Rainy Day, Dream Away," (1968)
"Still Raining, Still Dreaming
"Up From the Skies," (1968)
"Voodoo Chile," (1968)

IRON BUTTERFLY
(All songs published by Cotillion Music–Ten East/Itasca Music.)

"In-A-Gadda-Da-Vida," D. Ingle (1968)
"In the Time of Our Lives," Ingle-Bushy (1969)
"Lonely Boy," D. Ingle (1968)
"Most Anything You Want," D. Ingle (1968)
"Stamped Ideas," Ingle-Deloach (1968)

JANIS JOPLIN

"Kozmic Blues," Joplin-Mekler, Strong Arm-Wingate Music
   (1969)
"Try," Ragovoy-Taylor, Ragmar Music (1968)
"Turtle Blues," J. Joplin, Cheap Thrills Music (1968)

JEFFERSON AIRPLANE
(All songs by P. Kantner, Icebag Corp.)

"The Ballad of You & Me & Pooneil," (1967)
"Martha," (1967)
"Rejoyce," (1967)

THE RASCALS
(All songs published by Slacsar Publishing Co.)

"A Beautiful Morning," Cavaliere-Brigati (1968)
"Come On Up," F. Cavaliere (1966)
"How Can I Be Sure," Cavaliere-Brigati (1967)
"Love Is a Beautiful Thing," Cavaliere-Brigati (1966)
"People Got to Be Free," Cavaliere-Brigati (1968)

OTIS REDDING
(All songs published by East Publishing Co.)

"A Tribute to a King," Bell-Jones (1968)
"Chained and Bound," O. Redding (1964)
"Good for Me," Redding-Green (1966)
"Hawg for You," O. Redding (1966)
"I'm Sick Y'All," Redding-Cropper-Porter (1966)
"I Want to Thank You," O. Redding (1964)
"Little Miss Strange," N. Redding (1968)
"More Than Words Can Say," Floyd-Jones (1966)
"The Dock of the Bay," Cropper-Redding (1968)

THE ROLLING STONES
(All songs by Jagger-Richard, Gideon Music.)

"Heart of Stone," (1965)
"Lady Jane," (1966)
"Please Go Home," (1966)
"Satisfaction," (1965)
"The Lantern," (1967)

SANTANA

"Black Magic Woman," P. Green, Murbo Publishing Co. (1968)
"Oye Como Va," T. Puente, Planetary Music (1963)

SEALS & CROFT

"Summer Breeze," Seals & Croft, Warner Brothers Publishing
    (1971)

SIMON & GARFUNKEL
(All songs by P. Simon, Charing Cross Music.)

"A Hazy Shade of Winter," (1966)
"Big Bright Green Pleasure Machine," (1966)
"Bookends," (1968)
"Fakin' It," (1968)
"Mrs. Robinson," (1968)
"Patterns," (1965)
"Punky's Dilemma," (1968)
"Scarborough Fair/Canticle," (1966)
"Someday, One Day," (1966)

SLY & THE FAMILY STONE
(All songs by S. Stewart, Viva Music.)

"Everyday People," (1968)
"Hot Fun in the Summertime," (1969)
"I'm on a Trip to Your Heart," (1968)
"Life," (1968)
"Stand," (1969)

THE SUPREMES
(All music published by Jobete Music.)

"Everything Is Good About You," Grant-Whitfield-Holland
    (1966)
"Get Ready," W. Robinson (1965)
"I'm Losing You," Grant-Whitfield-Holland (1966)
"My World Is Empty Without You," Dozier-Holland (1965)
"You Keep Me Hanging On," Dozier-Holland (1966)

JAMES TAYLOR
(All songs by James Taylor, Blackwood Music.)

"Fire and Rain," (1969)
"Knocking Round the Zoo," (1969)
"Night Owl," (1970)
"Rainy Day Man," (1969)
"Something in the Way She Moves," (1968)
"Sunshine, Sunshine," (1968)
"Sweet Baby James," (1970)
"Takin' It In," (1969)

JIMMY WEBB (All songs by Jimmy Webb, Rivers Music.)

"By the Time I Get to Phoenix," (1967)
"Dream/Pax/Nepenthe," (1967)
"If I'd Been a Different Man," (1968)
"Magic Garden," (1967)
"Orange Air," (1967)
"Prologue," (1967)
"Summer's Daughter," (1967)
"The Girl's Song," (1967)
"Up, Up and Away," (1967)

WEBBER-RICE
(All songs by Webber-Rice, Leeds Music, 1970)

Jesus Christ Superstar,
   "Everything's All Right"
   "Hosanna"
   "Superstar"

THE WHO (Music published by Tro-Essex Music.)

"I Can See for Miles," G. Townsend (1967)
"Whiskey Man," J. Entwhistle (1967)

MISCELLANEOUS (Group not definite.)

"California Dreaming," J. Phillips, Wingate Music (1965)
"Child of Clay," Maresca-Curtis, Ernie Maresca, Inc. (1967)
"Steppin' Stone," Boyce-Hart, Screen Gems-Columbia (1966)

Traditional Compositions (Listed By Composer)

BARTÓK, BELA

Fourteen Bagatelles, Boosey & Hawkes
Mikrokosmos, Boosey & Hawkes
   "Fourths"
   "Minor Seconds, Major Sevenths"
   "Whole-Tone Scale"

DEBUSSY, CLAUDE

Afternoon of a Faun, International Music Co.
Children's Corner, Elkan-Vogel, Inc.
En blanc et noir, Elkan-Vogel, Inc.
Six epigraphes antiques, Elkan-Vogel, Inc.
The Engulfed Cathedral, Elkan-Vogel, Inc.

GRIFFES, CHARLES

Four Roman Sketches, G. Schirmer, Inc.

HONEGGER, ARTHUR

King David, E.C. Schirmer
Symphony No. 5, Editions Salabert
Horace Victorieux, G. Ricordi

KOECHLIN, CHARLES

Sonate pour piano et hautbois, Editions Salabert

MILHAUD, DARIUS

Chansons bas, Associated Music
Les Euménides, Theodore Presser
Les Choephores, Theodore Presser
La Délivrance de Thésée, Theodore Presser

RAVEL, MAURICE

Concerto for Piano and Orchestra, Elkan-Vogel, Inc.
Gaspard de la nuit, Elkan-Vogel, Inc.
String Quartet, International Music Co.
Valses, nobles et sentimentales, Elkan-Vogel, Inc.

RESPIGHI, OTTORINO

The Pines of Rome, G. Ricordi

RIEGGER, WALLINGFORD

Symphony No. 3, Associated Music Pub.

SATIE, ERIK

Gymnopédie No. 1, G. Schirmer, Inc.

SCHÖNBERG, ARNOLD

Suite for Clavier, Op. 25, "Menuett", Belmont Music Pub.

SCRIABIN, ALEXANDER

Desir, C.F. Peters

STRAVINSKY, IGOR

The Rite of Spring, Boosey and Hawkes
Petrouchka, Boosey and Hawkes

VAUGHAN WILLIAMS, RALPH

Pastoral Symphony, G. Schirmer, Inc.

Publisher's Addresses

Abigail Music Ltd.
67 Brook St.
London, W.1., England

Arch (Schroeder) Music Co.
25 West 56th St.
New York, N.Y. 10019

Associated Music Publishers
609 Fifth Ave.
New York, N.Y. 10017

Aurelius Music
10680 W. Pico Blvd.
Los Angeles, Cal. 90064

Belmont Music Publishers
P.O. 49961
Los Angeles, Cal. 90049

Berna Music Inc.
215 La Cienega Blvd.
Beverly Hills, Cal. 90211

Blackwood Music Inc.
1650 Broadway
New York, N.Y. 10019

Blue Book Music Co.
403 Chester Ave.
Bakersfield, Cal. 93301

Blue Seas-Jac Music Co.
Parkside, Knightsbridge
London, S.W.1., England

Boosey & Hawkes
30 W. 57th St.
New York, N. Y. 10010

Casserole Music Corp.
1700 Broadway
New York, N.Y. 10019

Charing Cross Music
40 E. 54th St.
New York, N.Y. 10022

Cotillion Music Inc.
1841 Broadway
New York, N.Y. 10023

Dwarf Music Inc.
Box 69, Prince Station
New York, N.Y. 10012

Dynatone Publishing Co.
1540 Brewster Ave.
Cincinnati, Ohio 45207

East Publishing Co.
926 McLemore Ave.
Memphis, Tenn. 38106

Elkan-Vogel Inc.
c/o Theodore Presser
Presser Place
Bryn Mawr, Pa. 19010

Ernie Maresca Inc.
165 W. 46th St.
New York, N.Y. 10030

Famous Music Corp.
1 Gulf-Western Plaza
New York, N.Y. 10019

Gideon Music Inc.
Time & Life Bldg.
1271 Ave. of Americas
New York, N.Y. 10019

Giving Room Music Inc.
55 Liberty St.
New York, N.Y. 10005

Gold Hill Music
55 Liberty St.
New York, N.Y. 10005

Guerilla Music Inc.
55 Liberty St.
New York, N.Y. 10005

Harrisongs Music Ltd.
3 Savile Row
London, N.1, England

Icebag Corporation
527 Madison Ave., Suite 317
New York, N.Y. 10022

International Music Co.
511 Fifth Ave.
New York, N.Y. 10017

Irving Music Co.
1416 North La Brea Ave.
Hollywood, Cal. 90048

Ja-Ma Music Co.
1330 Ave. of Americas
New York, N.Y. 10019

Jobete Music Co.
2457 Woodward Ave.
Detroit, Michigan 48201

Joint Music Inc.
444 Madison Ave.
New York, N.Y. 10022

Jondora Music Co.
10th St. & Parker
Berkeley, Cal. 94710

Leeds Music Corp.
445 Park Ave.
New York, N.Y. 10022

Murbo Publishing Co.
136 W. 52nd St.
New York, N.Y. 10019

Nipper Music Co.
962 N. La Cienega Blvd.
Los Angeles, Cal. 90069

Northern Songs, Ltd.
71-75 New Oxford St.
London, W.C.1, England

C.F. Peters Corp.
371 Park Ave. S.
New York, N.Y. 10016

Planetary Music Publishers
17 W. 60th St.
New York, N.Y. 10023

Theodore Presser
Presser Place
Bryn Mawr, Pa. 19010

Ragmar Music Inc.
353 W. 48th St.
New York, N.Y. 10036

C. Ricordi
c/o Belwin Mills
116 W. 61st St.
New York, N.Y. 10023

Rivers Music Co.
8923 Sunset Blvd.
Los Angeles, Cal. 90069

Rodra Music Co.
215 La Cienega Blvd.
Beverly Hills, Cal. 90211

Editions Salabert
575 Madison Ave.
New York, N.Y. 10017

Sea Lark-Yameta Co.
25 W. 56th St.
New York, N.Y. 10019

E.C. Schirmer
112 South St.
Boston, Mass. 02111

G. Schirmer Inc.
866 Third Ave.
New York, N.Y. 10022

Screen Gems-Columbia
6744 NE 4th Ave.
Miami, Fla. 33138

Salcsar Publishing Co.
444 Madison Ave.
New York, N.Y. 10022

Strong Arm-Wingate Music Co
1330 Ave. of Americas
New York, N.Y. 10019

Tamerlane Music Inc.
6290 Sunset Blvd.
Hollywood, Cal. 90028

Tro-Essex Music Inc.
Suite 1406,
10 Columbus Circle
New York, N.Y. 10019

Venice Music Corp.
8300 Santa Monica Blvd.
Hollywood, Cal. 90069

Viva Music Inc.
6922 Hollywood Blvd.
Hollywood, Cal. 90028

Warner Brothers Publishers
1230 Ave. of Americas
New York, N.Y. 10020

Wingate Music Corp.
1300 Ave. of Americas
New York, N.Y. 10019

M. Witmark & Sons
c/o Warner Bros. Pub.
1230 Ave. of Americas
New York, N.Y. 10020

Index